OUT OF
RED
DARKNESS

OUT OF
RED
DARKNESS

REPORTS
FROM THE
COLLAPSING
SOVIET EMPIRE

TREVOR
FISHLOCK

JOHN MURRAY

© Trevor Fishlock 1992

First published in 1992
by John Murray (Publishers) Ltd,
50 Albemarle Street, London W1X 4BD

A catalogue record for this book is available from the British Library

ISBN 0–7195–5004–1

Typeset in 11/13 pt Times by Wearside Tradespools, Boldon, Tyne and Wear, England
Printed and bound in Great Britain by Biddles of Guildford

For Penny

Contents

Plates

All photographs are by the author.

Preface

Moscow became an addictive drug for many foreign correspondents, a mixture of adrenalin and deadline-induced sweat, stirred with the excitement of being close to the whirlwind, with perhaps a dash of vodka. There was such an intensity in living there that it seemed to me on many days that we had the extraordinary for breakfast, amazement for lunch and astonishment for dinner. On leave, the Moscow stimulus withdrawn, we became jellies.

Much of our time was spent in our offices, trying to make sense and order of confusion and contradiction, trying to get the phone to work, but for me the most rewarding part of it all was the travelling, in and out of Moscow, meeting people, talking, and simply watching what went on in the streets and markets. It was not without risk: a large metal panel detached itself from a building one day and fell three yards in front of me. In my safer daily walk in the exercise yard of the park near my home I almost always saw some small scene, some human detail, that added to my knowledge of Russia. This book is mostly the product of the listening and watching aspect of my enjoyable time in Moscow. It is not a political chronicle, although momentous political events form the background. It is, in part, a funnel for the stories that ordinary Russians told me; and Lithuanians, Latvians, Estonians, Ukrainians, Georgians, Uzbeks, Armenians and Azerbaijanis, too. I met many of these people quite by chance, the correspondent in the form of a bagatelle ball. I received great kindness from strangers, from people who put themselves out to show me the reality of their lives; and I hope that the friendships formed will endure.

During my time in the Soviet Union the empire was being shaken like a tree in a storm. There was no doubt that it would crash. It was a question of how and when. I was moved by many of the events I witnessed, by the immense courage of ordinary people, who faced death, who demonstrated to arrogant planners that for all the plans and systems and 'the logic of history' the individual was not puny, that people counted, that truth could defeat lies.

Much of this book was written before the attempted coup, while Gorbachev, a remarkable man rather than a great man, a prisoner himself of his history, still held the reins of runaway horses. In just a few hours all those communist mountains of words and books and turgid speeches were blown away. Lenin retreated to the Finland Station, his legacy turmoil and waste.

I had to draw the line somewhere and so St Petersburg is Leningrad in most of this narrative. Indeed, the journey from Leningrad to St Petersburg is partly what the story is about. I have respected the wishes of those who asked me to disguise their names because at the time they talked to me they felt there were risks. As I have indicated, I owe much to ordinary people who revealed to me their warmth and also their pain. I am indebted to friends and colleagues who taught me much about the Soviet Union. Robin Lodge, with whom I shared several Soviet reporting adventures, kindly ran the proofs through his expert net. Penny, who herself saw and reported some of the dramas in the Baltic countries, was, throughout it all, and as ever, my right hand.

Prologue

Suddenly we were tumbling from the car and heading towards the gunfire, flinching and stumbling in the darkness of that icy January night in Lithuania in 1991. There was screaming and shouting. Rifles stuttered at people at close range, killing them, wounding them in their dozens. Thick white smoke rolled across the grassy slope and figures were running in and out of it, staggering and panting. Tanks roared and snorted, backing and wheeling. The thunderous shocking bang of a tank gun ripped the night apart and the ground trembled.

People jabbed at the notebook in my hand, gasping out what they had seen and what they were seeing, begging and commanding that it should all be recorded. White, taut faces glimpsed in the burst of a flare were flecked with mud, some with blood. A searchlight swivelled, seeking us out, and we crouched in a scrum, drawing breath together, smelling the earth, feeling naked and vulnerable.

A young woman, calm and admirable, spoke in a clear even voice of the killing she had seen. Her face was silver in the flickering light. She grasped my arm and looked directly into my eyes. Make sure, she said, that people outside are made aware of all this, that what the soldiers are doing to us is not forgotten or buried. Tell the truth before the communists tell their lies.

We scrambled down the slope to the road. A crowd had gathered around a tank, remonstrating, shaking puny fists as if at some malevolent scaly foul-breathed monster. The dark olive machine had already crushed someone under its tracks. It was throbbing and stinking. Its turret swung menacingly and the long barrel of the gun rose over us. Then a machine gun slowly turned, the muzzle moving over our faces in baleful inspection.

We went to the hospital where the floor was slippery with blood and bloody-aproned doctors worked frantically. There were desperate eyes, shouts of pain, whispers of grief. Two young men lay lifeless on soaked stretchers on the floor, their faces waxy, one with the back of his head shot away. These were the deaths that the army so earnestly wanted to bring about, the Kremlin fist smashing mouths talking of freedom and of change.

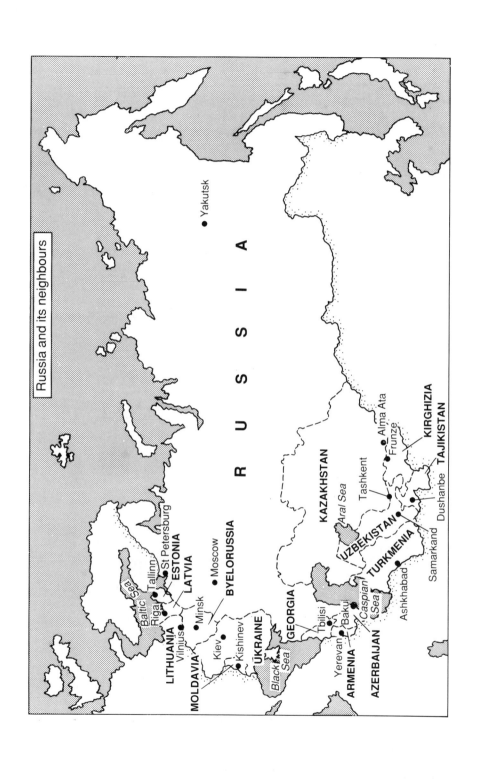

Russia and its neighbours

1

RED SQUARE

Tanks rocked and rattled over the dark cobbles, steel crunching on glinting granite, moving from left to right as we watched, in our compound a few yards from Lenin's tomb. Gorbachev smelt them. Blue exhaust stung the nostrils as it drifted in the cold morning air to the high swallowtail battlements of the Kremlin wall. It hung in smoky wreaths around the busts of Soviet heroes and leaders in front of their burial places in the wall.

Long lines of troops marched by, purposeful and grim. Cymbals clashed and boots crashed in goosestep rhythm. Helmeted heads jerked right like the sudden rippling snap of a venetian blind and the chins of raw rigid faces jutted upwards in salute to the line of leaders on the balcony of the mausoleum. Generals with boiled red faces looked on, barrel-shaped like a set of Russian dolls, in their long blue greatcoats. Crowned with braided caps as large as ranch frying pans and encrusted with golden epaulettes and gingerbread lapels, they were a picture of martial couture. Each left breast displayed what looked like a trayful of medals taken from a numismatist's window, each right breast a whole constellation of stars. The decorations were so abundant they spilled over the broad golden belts cinching aldermanic bellies.

Lenin looked down upon his legacy. Across the square his gigantic carmine portrait hung on the Victorian Gothic façade of GUM, the huge shopping arcade. The artist had given him a quizzical expression, and a celebratory striped tie. It was the morning of 7 November 1990, anniversary of the 1917 Revolution, of the day on which Russia's infant democracy was strangled; of the day Lenin found that taking power in the Russian empire through his almost accidental and almost bloodless coup was, as he remarked, as easy as picking up a feather.

But on this particular morning there was only a lingering vestige of an idea that the anniversary of the founding of the Soviet communist regime was worth celebrating. On the far side of the square were faces inured to defeat, pressed men who could think of better factory outings than this and better songs to sing. The times were too full of indignities for celebration, too full of want. The day before the parade a Russian acquaintance had told me about his recent trip to western Germany. 'What stayed in my mind', he said, 'was the way the people smiled, the way they carried themselves, confident. Look at the way we walk, dragging our feet, slouched, afraid to look each other in the eye. Smile? We have forgotten how to.' I asked him if he would watch the parade on television. He snorted.

The rot and disillusion could hardly be concealed. Gorbachev was overlord of a dying planet lit by a watery sun. Nations within the Soviet pale hacked at their gyves. In keeping with the times Moscow lay under the sombre cloud which seemed such an unrelieved feature of that tense and desperate winter – as if under the dome of a great wok.

In the half-hour walk from my home to Red Square I saw that the streets themselves bore witness to the shrivelling of the faith. The Communist Party had always ensured that on Revolution Day the city's face was well rouged, with masses of red bunting and exhortatory slogans urging people to greater glories. But now the harvest of flags was noticeably meagre. The dye seemed to have run from the banners. The days of socialist mafficking had waned and the old rituals were threadbare. The feather had become a leaden burden.

The slogan-mongers still invoked Lenin's name and loyally blew upon the cold coals of his works, but there was no mistaking the half-heartedness in the atmosphere, the sound of feet shuffling in embarrassment, the sense of decay, of loss of purpose. I could not possibly have imagined the events which would follow, but such was the feeling of a closing curtain that, as I wrote at the time, it seemed reasonable to wonder whether the Red Square Revolution Day parade had reached the end of its run after seven decades.

★   ★   ★

Gorbachev's immediate dilemmas sprang from his attempts to make a racehorse out of a rhinoceros. He took power in 1985 as a reformer: he had seen the Kremlin balance sheet and knew that the economy was rotting. Unable to feed itself or to afford its huge army, the country was on the edge of catastrophe. But his prescription was fatally flawed. He said that the communist system, the central command economy managed by the massive machinery of the state, could be reformed and made efficient, that a sense of purpose could be revived and the Union remain a single congregation. He soon ran into the essential contradiction: the Soviet system was in such a disastrous condition that it was beyond mere repair or overhaul. Genuine reform would have to be root-and-branch to have any effect, so radical that there would be no communist framework left. To attempt such a reform would be an astonishing repudiation of communism, the Revolution, Lenin and the sacred past.

Gorbachev was not the man for such a disavowal. He himself had once talked of the Soviet empire lasting a thousand years, an echo of the old Russian messianism, of the idea that with the Revolution the Bolsheviks were fulfilling a manifest destiny to change the world, to recast mankind. Gorbachev, raised in the communist orthodoxy, believed in Lenin's Revolution and the sanctity of the empire. He rose in a political and administrative apparatus in which lies were the ramparts of power and deceit the currency of government. His mentor was Andropov, the ruthless and treacherous Kremlin proconsul in Hungary at the time of the 1956 uprising, boss of the KGB for fifteen years, hounder of dissidents. But Andropov had observed how the spores of the Soviet rot propagated themselves in the lazy, hazy days of Brezhnev when nothing was done and millions of party members and bureaucrats wallowed in the muddle. Andropov poked about with a reformist stick and alarmed the old drones. The actions of his protégé, Gorbachev, alarmed them more.

If the old guard thought of change at all they thought of it in terms of applying more discipline, of tightening rather than loosening. They did not think the Soviet structure itself required examination: it had been erected scientifically, according to the laws of history and the precepts of Lenin. But a reformer inevitably raises questions about the status quo, about the integrity of the entire system.

It was here that Gorbachev stumbled and precipitated the terminal crisis of the empire. He never intended wholesale reform, or the ending of communist rule, or the freeing of the conquered Soviet republics. He proposed modest reforms, a little more land for the people to cultivate as they wished, a little encouragement of small-scale private businesses (known as co-operatives to avoid giving ideological offence), some autonomy in the huge state enterprises, some economic self-rule in the republics. It was intended as reform on a rein, and Gorbachev remained firmly opposed to private property. To stimulate a people made listless and indifferent by communism he permitted a greater freedom of the press and encouraged political debate and the holding of elections. His aim was a more humane, civilised and open society, one that could look the West in the eye – but a communist-controlled society nevertheless, not a democratic one.

The problem was that in this hot-house the democratic idea flowered. Opposition to the worn and corrupt Soviet system grew rapidly, with calls for real economic reform and something decent to eat. From a number of the Soviet republics came insistent demands for independence. Gorbachev was confronted with his fallacy of a limited reform of communism on his own terms. The rhinoceros could not be a racehorse. The glowering hardliners in the army, the KGB and the party, the pillars of the Soviet state, saw that everything they believed in, power, privilege and empire, was at risk. The collapse of communist regimes in Europe in 1989 sent shivers to every hardliner's heart, an intimation of mortality.

Political turmoil was matched by economic chaos. At a time of open discussion of the possibility of a hardliners' coup, Gorbachev abandoned reform and showed his authoritarian hand. He joined the hard men who could think of only one remedy for the crisis: repression. By the time of the Revolution Day parade in 1990 the Soviet Union was foundering and the old dream of the socialist state lay dismasted.

In this inchoate swirl the people formed a seething conspiracy, millions spinning webs of deviousness to shape an endurable existence. Life had serrations of anarchy and strong aspects of fantasy. Satirists depicted the Soviet reality as a madhouse and agriculture as a plough drawn by a pantomime horse. Political direction seemed to follow the blue Moscow road signs whose contorted arrows suggested the troilist copulation of snakes. Political discourse sometimes had the ring of the transactions of a flat earth society. In an increasingly febrile atmosphere people showed an extraordinary interest in mysticism, soothsayers, hypnotists and other witch-doctors. There were numerous accounts of meetings with visitors from other planets. The horrible aftermath of the Chernobyl disaster, the drying up of the Aral Sea as a sacrifice to scientific production and the gross pollution of industrial cities engendered a deep suspicion of technology.

The bizarre became commonplace. A Soviet Frankenstein related that he had experimented with corpses, trying to bring them back to life. In forty cases, he said, the dead stood up and walked, but it had proved impossible to reanimate their brains. When blood ran short, prospective donors were lured to a Leningrad clinic by the promise of a pair of socks in exchange for 200 grams of blood; there was also a shortage of socks. Indeed, a man in one Russian town, despairing of finding socks in the shops, wrote bitterly to the Kremlin. An official responded, directing the man to a shop where he received a parcel of socks at Moscow's command. A Canadian radio station, unable to pay one of its regular Moscow contributors in cash, paid him in socks. A woman wrote to the Kremlin complaining about the lack of underwear for sale and was sent a parcel of knickers. In the city of Rostov-on-Don in southern Russia, newborn babies still received letters from the authorities welcoming them to the 'spectacular accomplishments of the world's most progressive society', presenting them with a medal inscribed with their year of birth, and urging them to set out on life 'to win like Lenin'. In 1990 there was a shortage of medals, and babies were given those left over from 1988.

In 1920 H. G. Wells, who visited Russia and interviewed Lenin, wrote: 'Ruin; that is the primary Russian fact at the present time.' More than seventy years on, it remains the primary fact.

★　　　　★　　　　★

Gorbachev, on the balcony of the tomb, wore the scarf, trilby and thick grey overcoat that gave him the appearance of a prosperous British provincial football club director. A line of ministers, high-ranking officials and service officers had distributed themselves to left and right of him. There was a time when this congregation on the granite quarterdeck was one of the representative images of the Soviet Union. Down the years those wintry faces of tyrants and dotards, faces in which there seemed not a calorie of warmth, were studied minutely for clues to the Kremlin's dark workings, to find who had fallen from the sledge and who had clambered on board.

I looked for Raisa Gorbachev. At the previous Revolution Day parade she had come over to our reporters' compound as bright and jaunty as a jay, her KGB guards ravens at her shoulder. She flashed her photogenic smile, autographed our pink admission tickets and chatted. She had a part to play. Personable, intelligent and fashion-ably-dressed, she was a bright accessory in Gorbachev's roadshow, serving his cause while he brought the Soviet Union from its cold war cave, altered political geography and made rivers run back-wards. In the West, where there was a cartoonists' idea that Soviet woman was a version of Shetland pony, Mrs Gorbachev's striking appearance was a glamorous surprise. American television pre-sented her as the equivalent of the White House First Lady. The story that she had an American Express card was probably untrue, but it was part of the package that seemed to make her less a creature from space and more a member of the sorority of shoppers.

No Soviet leader had ever had such a consort. Kremlin wives had hitherto kept a kind of purdah. The self-effacing wife of a commun-ist baron would be seen briefly by the public for the first and last time as a dumpy widow bending sorrowfully over the open coffin to kiss the marbled face. Mrs Gorbachev's visibility was a departure from tradition, effective abroad but viewed coolly by many at home. The gulf between the Kremlin and the people was wide; Mrs Gorbachev was a Kremlin duchess with the privileges of rank, married to the boss of a repressive system whose failures bowed the people. Only a few knew of her qualities as confidante and political support. 'My general', Gorbachev called her. She was for export, seen on television far more in the West than in the Soviet Union. *Pravda*, the Communist Party daily, was traditionalist. It published few photographs of her. It also adhered to the custom of depicting communist leaders as men without blemish, and dutifully airbrushed away the distinctive blaze on Gorbachev's forehead.

★ ★ ★

In November 1982 the Red Square spectacle of imperial might, the missiles and armour and marching legions, was the last chance, a few days before he died, for Brezhnev to sniff the tanks, the perfume of power. Brezhnev loved military swagger and medals. He had conferred on himself enough stars and orders to drag him to the bottom of the sea. A comedian used to ape him by walking on stage with medals stretching ridiculously down his jacket, and amid the laughter would turn his back to reveal another array. Brezhnev was posthumously stripped of one of his finest medals on the grounds that he had invented the wartime exploit for which he had presented it to himself. In a regime where deceit and fabrication were commonplace, it seemed one of the smaller crimes.

At the end of his life his glazed eyes looked out on a country stitched into one vast Soviet quilt. No one knew it then but his passing was the end of an age of certainty, of fat years that the communist barons would look back on with nostalgia. Now in Red Square the military swagger did not carry the same conviction and troops marched less in a celebration of Founder's Day, more in a stern assertion of military power in an empire feeling its age and beset by neuroses.

The watching generals were troubled, brooding on the collapse of certainties and of purpose, on the country's material decline and bankruptcy of spirit. They had known very different times and had been schooled in the idea that they were glorious defenders of the people, the shield of socialism, an instrument of the Communist Party, the vanguard of the grand idea of socialist revolution. Those articles of faith were constantly renewed and monitored by political officers lecturing in the Lenin Rooms in every barracks, warship and air base. It was not so long ago that the generals had had everything they wanted: respect, prestige, almost unlimited money (a quarter of the national budget), control of one of the world's greatest military machines; indeed, the centrally planned economy was directed towards military strength. Garrisons secured fifteen Soviet republics and a swathe of eastern Europe. The generals had a sense of an historic role and of purpose in facing the West. Now, however, the army was a cracked bell.

Disillusionment affected all ranks. In a few years almost everything career soldiers had taken for granted had been called into question: esteem, money, legends, glory, role and direction. In some parts of the Soviet Union that Revolution Day, generals staged parades against the wishes of the local people, who protested that the troops were armies of occupation. More cautious commanders held parades in their barracks and not on the streets, for fear of provoking the wrath of local inhabitants: resentment and volatility staked out limits to Moscow's writ.

A magazine-writer who interviewed a hundred women said that many girls did not like to be seen on the arm of a soldier: public regard for the services was declining and anti-military feeling was growing. Another magazine reported that some military men wore civilian clothes on the way to work because they felt embarrassed in their uniforms.

The war in Afghanistan had been unpopular with the public, and the poor treatment of returning veterans of the war had also created a pool of discontent. People were angered that the bodies of men killed in action were not treated with honour but regarded with embarrassment, to be disposed of furtively. Large numbers of young men, particularly in the Baltic and Caucasian republics, ignored the call-up. This was partly an assertion of nationalist spirit, a refusal to serve in the conqueror's army, and partly through fear of the widespread bullying and murder of recruits being revealed in the press and by protesting parents. Thousands were deserting. The army had never before encountered such anti-militarism and resistance to the call-up; nor had it ever had to deal with insistent questions about its role. It earned contempt for savagely attacking and killing women in Georgia in 1989 and for harassing the notably peaceful people of the Baltic countries.

Hardline officers were angry with Gorbachev. They blamed him for relaxing the official grip on the press, enabling newspapers to

expose army brutality and to criticise the military. They insisted that
the rebellious Balts be put in their place and that call-up resisters
and deserters be treated severely. They blamed Gorbachev for the
retreat from Afghanistan and for 'losing the empire' – doing nothing
while the communist regimes in Eastern Europe fell one by one and
Soviet troops meekly began their withdrawal. Many officers felt the
humiliation of defeat and fumed at the spectacle of Russian soldiers
in eastern Europe selling their uniforms to souvenir hunters and
scavenging in Berlin rubbish dumps for household goods. The
return of the troops exacerbated the already serious shortage of
housing for officers and non-commissioned officers. Middle-ranking
men committed to a military career felt that defence cuts left them
with an uncertain future. Some fumed when Moscow sided with the
United States in the Gulf war and deserted its old ally, Iraq.

Gorbachev confronted the army with the reality that the Soviet
Union was bankrupt and that the world had changed. He said the
forces had to become affordable and manageable. Many officers
acknowledged the sense of this. They could see something of the
real condition of the country from figures showing the large number
of recruits rejected because of poor physical condition, a reflection
of the bad food and health care in the population at large.

Military myths were being up-ended as complacency was shaken.
The forces had basked in the glow of victory in the Second World
War, known as 'the great patriotic war', the triumph of communism
over fascism, the preservation of Mother Russia at the cost of much
blood. In this finest hour, the legend went, the country was uniquely
united and selfless. Defeat of the Nazis was fashioned in popular
narrative as a vindication of the Soviet system. Victory was a theme
endlessly reworked in parades, books, television programmes and
the cinema. Older people still cling to the idea that victory was due
to the towering military genius of Stalin. In the more open press of
the Gorbachev years there emerged the unpalatable truth that
Stalin's destruction of the officer class had imperilled his country
and laid it open to invasion, and that the millions of war dead, the
legendary Soviet sacrifice, included many killed at his order.

On the forty-fifth anniversary of victory the generals held a grand
parade in Red Square, intended as a morale-booster in bewildering
times. They wanted to remind the public of the army's victorious

past and its present power. Above all, they fervently wished to win back respect and popularity. The parade was meant to celebrate the heroism and unity of purpose depicted in the colossal memorial statues and in the triumphant films. In the statues and on the screen the bayonets are turned outward, towards the hated invader, and there is resolution on every countenance: forty-five years on, the soldiers' purpose was not so clear and their bayonets were being turned inward, towards the inadequately-filled bellies of their fellow-citizens.

★   ★   ★

Red Square is where the long rutted roads of all Russia have their confluence. It has ever been a grand stage, a place of rendezvous, congregation and pageantry. Here you may see all the faces of Russia and its neighbours and hear many of their hundred languages. On these dark cobbles Siberia rubs shoulders with Samarkand and Baltic jostles Bering. Reindeer herders from Yakutia meet orchard workers from Georgia and Cossacks encounter Kazakhs. Coughing Ukrainian miners who will be lucky to reach fifty meet fig-brown Caucasians who boast of fathering at eighty and living to a hundred. Many of these tourists are making their first and perhaps their only visit to Moscow and there is much work for the photographers who earn a living on the square, setting up their stalls beneath large umbrellas. Everyone wants a souvenir to pin on a wall. The people stand in pairs and in groups, posing as stiffly solemn as Victorians. Old men stick out their chests to show their medals, bare their gold teeth and arrange their fur hats, Lenin caps or fedoras. The photographers frame them against the nine Ali Baba turbans of the Cathedral of St Basil the Blessed or against the Saviour's Tower of the Kremlin or the sullen cubist pile of Lenin's mausoleum.

Policemen strut and blow their whistles, sounding like demented budgerigars as they keep the strollers in order, guarding invisible lines on the cobbles. In Moscow it is easy to think that every tenth person is a policeman; and it is reckoned that there are as many policemen in Moscow and St Petersburg as there are in all Italy. They infest the streets, waggling their batons and stopping drivers for offences real or invented, both to keep order and to improve their meagre wages.

Whistles used to blow loudest of all when large black limousines sped along the avenues or rushed onto Red Square from the Saviour's Gate, bearing Communist Party aristocrats who sat hidden like Garbo behind the curtains. Muscovites were accustomed to this high speed assertion of rank. When Soviet newspapers reported that in England the Princess Royal had been prosecuted for speeding, readers were astonished. The first surprise was that a member of the élite drove her own car. The second was that a police officer felt confident enough to stop one of the Royal family and report her. The third was that a court convicted her. The wonders of a law-based society were of deep interest in a state where the privileged rode roughshod over the people and where the largely disreputable police knew their place.

The geographical and human enormity of which Red Square is the heart both stimulates and confounds imagination. It covers a sixth of the world's land mass, is two and a half times the size of the United States, seven times larger than India, ninety times larger than Britain. Texas would slip into its fob pocket. The distance from Baltic to Bering, almost 7,000 miles, covers eleven of the world's twenty-four time zones.

But much of the land is unblessed and little of its wealth is drawn from it with ease. No Eden, this. The failure throughout history of one harvest in three is stored in the Russian memory as are the rings in an ancient tree. Immense tracts of the land are so forbidding and hard, so unkind and even brutal to man where they are not uninhabitable, that much of the country seems like a vast lifeless moon.

Russia bends under the punishing burden of its north-ness. December, January and February hang like chains. Half of the territory lies north of the 60th parallel and two-fifths is permafrost, permanently frozen subsoil. A sixth is a swathe of treeless tundra and south of this stretches the taiga, the greatest single forest formation on earth, which in spring becomes a sea of glutinous mud. Across the Russian belly lies the broad cummerbund of steppe,

prairie land of such eye-aching vastness that you may fancy you can
see the curvature of the planet.

When poets put their ears to the ground in this region, they hear a
thrilling reverberation. Out of the centuries rolls the tympanic
thunder of the Devil's Horsemen, the Tartars, grandsons of Genghis
Khan, the brilliant Mongol mounted armies which conquered and
terrorised Russia after 1236 and held it for 250 years. They
deposited in the Russian mind an indelible mark and a shadow of
fear and, in Russian blood, a Tartar strain. For Russia is shaped in
part by its enigmatic Asian dimension, by its mightiest conquerors
as well as by what it has conquered. It is undoubtedly European and
the bulk of its people live in the Russian heartland west of the Ural
mountains, a region larger than India. But the Asian territory of
Russia beyond the Urals is four times larger than the heartland. The
exploration and colonisation of Siberia extended Russia to the
shores of the Pacific. This Asian component of the Slavic entity is
part of Russian uniqueness and ambivalence, exerting a force upon
culture and imagination as surely as the moon affects the sea.

★   ★   ★

Red Square's citadel, the Kremlin, is the hand which grasped the
reins of empire. The Kremlin lies at history's axis, a walled city of
palaces and painted halls and cathedrals and as perforated with
passages as an anthill, full of secret doors and priest's holes and
rusty-locked dungeons. From a distance its scintillating gilded
domes, cupolas and pinnacles give it the look of a fantastic box of
bedknobs and baubles, and in the changing light its walls shade from
cheek-pink to poppy, from liver to embers. *Kreml* means fortifica-
tion, and the first oak stockade was raised here above the Moscow
river in the twelfth century. The brick walls, up to sixteen feet thick
and commanded by twenty towers, were built by Italians in the
fifteenth century and enclose seventy acres of architectural splen-
dours and halls of government, as if Downing Street, Whitehall,
Buckingham Palace, St Paul's and yet more palaces and churches
were gathered within the precincts of the Tower of London.

The Kremlin's buildings and their decorations meet a Russian appetite, amounting to a craving, for magnificence. Trotsky, who did not visit the Kremlin until March 1918, said it seemed a paradoxical place to establish the stronghold of the revolutionary dictatorship. But he need not have worried – it was the perfect place, and the revolutionaries soon grew accustomed to it. It fitted like a glove. They and their successors continued its tradition as a theatre of violence, betrayal and madness, of secrecy, sycophancy and cruelty.

I paid a few dollars one day and joined a small tourist group led by a slim and pretty Russian guide. Whenever she turned to face and address us she rose upon a balletic tiptoe. 'This', she said, with a sweep of her arm, 'is the territory of the Kremlin.' She was a tape-recorder in an agreeable human form and whenever she made a mistake she rewound and edited herself. She pointed to the heaviest bell in the world, which stands broken and unrung beside Ivan the Great's bell tower. 'The Emperor Bell was casted in the seventeenth century and weighs twenty tons,' she said. She paused, tracked back and started again. 'The Emperor Bell was casted in the eighteenth century and weighs two hundred tons.' When we crossed the pink stones of Cathedral Square I was reminded that I once saw Gorbachev play the Intourist guide to Ronald Reagan here. Behind the president walked his aide, an officer carrying the black bag containing the codes that would launch America's nuclear weapons – some of which were doubtless targeted on that very square.

At the conclusion of our tour the guide stood on her toes and bade us farewell. An American in the group was puzzled. 'Is that it?' he asked his wife. 'So where's the Kremlin?' 'You're right in it,' she said. 'This is the Kremlin. You've been walking round it for two hours.'

It was hard not to feel sympathy for him. The prospect of a visit to the Kremlin seems to promise an insight into the secret heart of Russia, as if there might be one room, one artefact, that would provide enlightenment, an explanation. Although the visitor is able to penetrate the formidable walls, about four-fifths of the Kremlin remain closed, a secret place, the core of Churchill's 'riddle wrapped in a mystery inside an enigma'. To Russians and foreigners alike it has been for centuries the essence of Russia's contradictions:

the fulcrum of religious faith and of tyranny, its history reeking of incense and blood; its fantastic architecture, traditions and legends the ingredients of a lurid fairy tale, peopled by mad kings and poisoned princes and punctuated by head-choppings and other bedtime horrors. In Stalin's time it was closed, a forbidden city, a hall of mirrors where death warrants were taken in sheaves and men were unmanned in the vestibules of fear.

In the shadow of the Kremlin walls the square was the arena for the city's daily pageant and circus of robust commerce. It was always Red Square, red and beautiful being the same word in old Russian. Lady Londonderry, who visited Russia in 1836–7, remarked that 'St Petersburg is a magnificent town but it can never be the capital of Russia. Moscow is Russia with an Asiatic colouring . . . the lovely, half-Asiatic, half-European city captured my imagination.'

Travellers marvelled at the abundance at the heart of Russia. The Red Square market was a cornucopia of meat and game, barrels of fish, poultry and fruit. The stalls were piled with furs, cloth, carpets, gold, jewellery and the icons that Russians adored, all the treasures of Siberia and China, Persia, Afghanistan and the Middle East. There were the shouts of pedlars and beggars, the laughter of rough crowds milling around dancing bears and jugglers, the pipes and fiddles of itinerant musicians. In this teeming souk were crammed churches, bath houses and taverns. The stinking smoky taverns were so uproarious in the seventeenth century that the Grand Prince of Moscow prohibited the sale of vodka, beer and tobacco and ordered that transgressors should be beaten or have their noses slit.

He was another in that long line of rulers – princes, khans, tsars and commissars – who have sought to bring order to a land too large for one man to know well, too harsh and intractable to be bent completely to one man's will. Rulers down the centuries have sought to reconcile the contradictions of the Russian sprawl, its human variety and innate and incorrigible unruliness.

There is something in Russia that has made men want to kick it and shake it and reform it. They have railed at its slovenliness and backwardness and shiftlessness. Lenin, for one, had a horror of that streak in his countrymen personified by Oblomov, the lazy hero of Goncharov's novel. Russian history has been marked by volcanic eruptions of reformist energy, by the sound of protesting square pegs being hammered into round holes, by the roars of exasperated leaders.

There was Father Tsar, then Father Lenin and Father Stalin, a belief that Russia could be managed only by strong autocrats, by giants accorded a mantle of divinity. The blows struck by Peter the Great reverberate still. During the years from 1689 to 1725 he took his country by the scruff of its wretched neck and applied a manic energy to his attempts to bring it up to date with advancing Europe. He suddenly and bizarrely snipped off the beards of every nobleman in his court. It was a shocking act: to the boyars, the noblemen, their beards were their sacred adornment. To Peter they were the symbols of the self-satisfied conservatism he detested. He set up beard checkpoints at the gates of Moscow, complete with barbers, to ensure that no man except humble peasant or priest went whiskered into the city. Some noblemen, grieving and humiliated, placed their shorn beards under their tear-stained pillows.

Gorbachev joined the ranks of exasperated leaders. He, like the Grand Prince, attacked a Russian tradition, ordering restrictions on the sale of vodka and other liquor. It was an action that had damaging economic and political effects. It made Gorbachev unpopular, another high-handed Kremlin authoritarian denying men their solace. The restrictions led to the rapid growth of a black market in drink and a substantial loss to the exchequer on the liquor tax. Where men could not get vodka they made and bought moonshine, often dangerous. Illicit stills sprang up everywhere, causing a serious sugar shortage which disrupted the traditional summer bottling of fruit and the making of jam, infuriating the women. In one Russian town women complained that they could not get eau-de-cologne because the local drunks were buying it all. There was rioting in some places when the vodka ran out. It all showed how out of touch were the leaders in the Kremlin, imagining they could eliminate by decree a vice with complex roots, thinking they could bully people into new habits.

★   ★   ★

After the Revolution the communists swept Red Square clean of trade and drove out much of its everyday human traffic. The square reflected the new times and became sterile and controlled, a metaphor for the totalitarian heart, a stage for orchestrated celebrations of the success of socialism where carefully vetted crowds marched, cheered and sang. Sometimes the cheering was enhanced by recorded hurrahs played over loudspeakers, canned adulation, making up for a widespread lack of public enthusiasm for communism noted by Lenin himself in his gloomy review of the Bolshevik achievement four years after the Revolution.

It took seventy years; but at last, in Gorbachev's time, the people were impatient and bold enough to show their feelings. During the May Day procession of 1990 Gorbachev and his coterie looked down in dismay from Lenin's tomb on a scene that was almost surreal: demonstrators, hardly able to believe their own daring, punched their fists into the air and shouted their frustration with communist rule only yards from Lenin's bones. Shame, shame, they cried, down with socialism, down with the KGB, down with the cult of Lenin, down with the empire of red fascism. A bearded priest stalked to the mausoleum brandishing a dramatic figure of a crucified Christ and called out to Gorbachev: 'Christ has risen, Mikhail Sergeyevich.'

Gorbachev was reminded by the demonstrators that for the Soviet Union it was very late in the day. He drummed his fingers on the parapet. Then he and the others turned on their heels and strode in memorable exit from the balcony as the crowd jeered their departing backs. The wheel of history had turned. May Day lunch in the Kremlin was no festival.

Gorbachev once insisted, in an anguished proclamation of destiny, that the Soviet Union was impossible to break up. He himself vowed he would be a communist to his dying day. How, he asked aloud, could he turn his back on the beliefs his father and grandfather had struggled for? As if he had heard a tocsin, he told Ukrainians and Byelorussians that 'We Slavs must stick together.' I met old men who asked if this tawdry state was what they had worked and fought for. The communist search for unicorns had ended in disillusion and its cover story had been exposed by gigantic failures. The communist experience was as ugly as any dark epoch in

Russia's history; the threads running through most of it were cruelty, injustice and dishonesty.

It has been argued, by Soviet apologists in the West too, that there is a balance sheet in which slaughter and tyranny should be set against epic social and industrial achievements; that, in the monstrous proposition, eggs had to be broken to make an omelette. The communists did not even make an omelette. There is no redeeming feature. Nothing good was built on the bones. On a poisoned and impoverished wasteland, ill-fed people, in declining health, scrounge for food, their motif the queue, the shuffling millipede of degradation.

Lenin – and his successors, into the 1980s – attacked skill, passion, loyalty, family life, humour and originality, and encouraged betrayal and spite. They made cynics of millions and reduced them to the indignities of dependence. The people look back at a chronicle of wasted years. The suppression of truth and history leave a population bereaved, filling in the gaps in their past, orphans searching for parents. Stalin was blamed, of course, but the Stalinist machinery stayed in place and its supporters were prepared to use force to keep it there.

★   ★   ★

The absurdities and restrictions of their existence drove many people to choose an exile of the mind. Ignoring the Soviet Union as much as possible they made their lives in a small and trusted circle of friends, nests in which their humanity survived. In cramped flats and shared kitchens they found protection and intimacy. 'The kitchen is the room of truth in a Soviet home,' Vitaly Korotich, then editor of the popular magazine *Ogonyok*, said to me:

the most important room, where people open their hearts, where literature is born, where forbidden songs are sung, where a man can talk properly to a woman. The authorities were never able to bug every kitchen in the land. The kitchen is a place of normality.

In public we have had to protect ourselves and say what a wonderful Soviet system we have. In the kitchen, among our friends, we admit the reality of life. I tell my writers that I will not accept a thing from them that they would not discuss in the kitchen. Only in the kitchen is there truth, and the search for truth is part of the struggle in our country to restore dignity. Over the years many have been arrested and executed for uttering half a word of truth. I can tell you, judging from all the letters I receive, that most people in our country do not want riches. They crave normality, a normal society, an ordinary life. Millions are recovering from the illusion that if they connect the radio and all its propaganda to an empty refrigerator they will be well fed and happy.

Humour, sardonic and subversive, helped people to deal with the disparity between reality and propaganda. ('Waiter, this plate is wet.' – 'That's your soup.') The official fictions on the air and in the press were supported by the ubiquitous slogans, by Lenin totems, and by regiments of statues cast in the Soviet Heroic mould, the men muscular and the women abundant, reaching for glory. The statues were cast first, the deeds were to follow, but the statues became caryatids supporting an edifice of lies. Those at the permanent Exhibition of Economic Achievements in Moscow, for example, raise hosannas to plentiful harvests and industrial triumphs and stand guard over a forlorn display of products rarely available. I was struck by a case with a mountain of paper-clips bearing a label showing that factories had reached paper-clip production levels set by central planners. Around the golden statues and spectacular fountains there drifted the smoke of primitive fires. Men roasted lumps of tough gristly meat and dished them up on paper plates with gobs of tomato sauce.

A Russian friend in his early twenties said: 'We were all taught at school that our country was the promised land and that other countries lagged far behind us. Then one day a boy brought a toy car to show us. It had been made in the West. We saw at once that it was far superior to anything we had seen here. So we realised then, as small boys, that we had been lied to. Nothing was ever the same again.'

The American journalist John Reed, who witnessed the 1917
Revolution, declared that 'Russian people no longer need priests to
pray them into heaven. On earth they were building a kingdom
more bright than any heaven had to offer.' In 1931, the year
Gorbachev was born, a book was published in Moscow which told
children about the realisation of the communist dream.

> After we build socialism [it said] all will have equally healthy
> faces. There will no longer be dwarves – people with ex-
> hausted, pale faces. Healthy strong giants, red-cheeked and
> happy – such will be the new people. Down with the kitchen!
> We are going to destroy this little penitentiary! We shall free
> millions of women from housework! We shall construct new
> socialistic cities in which there will be happy singing of birds
> and the calm refreshing voices of trees instead of the present
> clang and rumble and roar!

The book urged children to 'destroy ten marmots a year in the
regions infested with these animals . . . to catch or destroy five rats
and ten mice . . . to destroy bedbugs, cockroaches and flies in
500,000 homes.'

While children were encouraged to exterminate vermin the
authorities were exterminating people, obliterating the ablest farmers, destroying their own seed corn of agricultural knowledge and
commitment to the land, fouling their own nest, creating huge new
tribes of fearful unhealthy serfs and dwarves while proclaiming that
they were building a paradise populated with red-cheeked giants.

From Lenin's tomb the leaders looked towards the majestic bulk of
GUM, the state universal store, 275 yards long and three storeys
high, a crystal palace enclosing three glass-and-iron arcades and
galleries of shops. When it was built a century ago to replace
fifteenth-century trading arcades, it was at the bustling centre of a
burgeoning merchant city buzzing with the life of factories, theatres,
churches, galleries, restaurants, bars and cafés. After the Revolu-

tion the communists established GUM as the state's consumer showcase. Today it reflects the poverty of Soviet rule, the failure to provide, the shortages of almost every commodity. It is an epitaph to an extinguished commercial spirit.

One day I saw tense and anxious people, kept in order by two policemen, gathered outside a jewellery shop in GUM. They were waiting to buy thin gold chains, something of value in a society which despised its own currency. There was an ugly moment when some of the restless queue turned on a man in the line. 'Foreigner!' they cried. 'Why should he go in? Get him out.' The man slunk away. Then for some reason the police abruptly shut the shop doors. There was an eruption of anger but it subsided and the crowd drifted away, swearing. A shifty black marketeer sidled up to people and began offering gold chains.

At the end of one of the arcades there was a shop which provided an echo of the handsomely stocked textile stores of the late nineteenth century. This was the Benetton store, filled with expensive woollens, the sort of clothing that most Russians could only dream of. People were pressing their noses to the windows but they could not get in. A notice on the door said that only credit card holders could shop there: Soviet citizens did not have credit cards. A policeman guarded the door. People stared through the window at the engrossing spectacle of foreign tourists shopping with credit cards. In another shop was an exhibition of Lego models labelled 'Millions of children all over the world play with Lego – when will your kids get their kits?' For many Russian parents, the impoverished in pursuit of the unobtainable, it was a good question.

I visited Christian Dior's new shop near Red Square. It was fenced off with steel railings and the shop was entered through a narrow gap where a young woman checked that customers had an admission card, a ticket from their trade union branch. A red-faced policeman, bulky in black greatcoat and blue fur hat, guarded the glass doors. In the shop itself, in heavy contrast to the willowy assistants in cerise uniforms, were two more policemen. A notice stated that the shop was open that day only for people from the Frunzensky district of Moscow with admission cards. The attraction of the shop was that not only were cosmetics for sale, but they could be bought for roubles. Entry was limited to prevent a heavy siege.

Two women told me the cards issued by their union permitted them one hour of shopping, and they were buying for fifty others in their office as well as for themselves. They had thick wads of roubles. In spite of the difficulties and having to shop under the eye of the police, they thought themselves fortunate to have an hour away from work in a warm shop where they did not have to queue and they could be certain of buying something.

At the Estée Lauder shop close by, there was a different system. Again, the premises were fenced off with steel barriers and police were on guard. A long line of people waited stoically amid flurries of snow. A woman creeping slowly towards her goal said she had been waiting half an hour and calculated she would be inside in about another hour. 'I want toilet water,' she said. 'The prices are very high, but what to do? At least this shop is open to anyone who is prepared to queue and you don't need a ticket from your union as you do at Dior.'

I remarked to a man that he was a hero to be standing in the line. 'No,' he said. 'I'll only be a hero if I arrive home with the perfume.' His friend chimed in with a grin: 'You see how lucky we Russians are. This is a very happy experience for us. All we have to do is stand in the healthy fresh air for a couple of hours and then our dreams come true. In the West you do not have this feeling of achievement. So you see, the communist system is better.'

A woman emerged from the shop: she had bought two lipsticks and an eye-shadow. 'It was lovely,' she said, 'and the assistants were so polite it was amazing.' The Soviet system has chased manners underground, and people have grown accustomed to being treated with disdain by curmudgeonly clerks and shop assistants. A newspaper remarked that showing assistants how to be courteous would be as difficult as teaching them the acting technique of Stanislavsky. But the new cosmetics shops had nevertheless trained their people to be polite, had successfully deSovietised them.

So rapidly was the Soviet Union changing in the years I worked there that there were times when I felt we were on a diet of mustard, and we began to feel out-of-sorts if we did not have our regular dose of sensation. The word 'unprecedented' became worn with over-use.

It was hard to believe, for example, that a squalid encampment of hovels, not much larger than kennels, made from wood and cardboard, plastic and sacking, could spring up almost overnight behind St Basil's Cathedral on the edge of Red Square. The city authorities, newly-elected radicals, allowed the camp to stay. It would have been unthinkable a few months earlier. The two hundred inhabitants of the hovels called themselves 'the union of the persecuted' and had written out their woes on pieces of cardboard pinned to their shacks or hung by string around their necks. Pathetic grandmothers slept on the frozen mud surrounded by bewildered panda-eyed children and gaunt old men. A man sat, rigid with cold, clutching a placard – 'Brainless Bonehead Lenin' – in his blue fingers. Some of the people were Armenians, others Azerbaijanis, homeless refugees, together in wretchedness and at odds in the feud they now brought to the Kremlin door. A middle-aged unshaven Armenian man and a bedraggled Azerbaijani woman stood nose to nose in the mud, spluttering hatred at each other. 'Enemy!' snarled the man. 'Enemy!' He spat in the woman's face and tears rolled down her cheeks. Tourists spilled from the ugly Rossiya hotel nearby, pushing through the taxi drivers, black marketeers and other meat-flies who hang around Moscow hotel entrances, to stare at the dismal scene. Camera flash lit up the shacks. It was like a visit to Bedlam. As it grew darker the large red star on top of the Saviour's Tower in the Kremlin was switched on, a glowing symbol of Soviet power. A man squatting beside his shack carefully delineated the letters on a cardboard placard: 'Defend us from Soviet tyranny'.

Most of the world's cities have tidal deposits of poor, homeless and misfits, but until recently such wretchedness did not exist officially in the Soviet Union. When the weather grew very cold the authorities bulldozed the camp and moved its inhabitants. They would otherwise have frozen to death.

It was another sign of change that for the first time since the Revolution there were religious services in St Basil's and in one of the Kremlin cathedrals. The communists destroyed thousands of churches in their campaign against religion and ostentatiously converted some of the finest surviving ones into museums of atheism, or factories. The Russian Orthodox Church emerged from its struggle with communism battered, weakened, but alive.

The Orthodox faith is in the sinew and spirit of Russia, part of Russian distinctiveness. Its adoption ten centuries ago was an historic point of departure. Derived from Byzantium, from Constantinople rather than Rome, from East rather than West, it set Russia apart from the European mainstream. Prince Vladimir of Kiev accepted it as a means of accelerating the spread of civilisation among his pagan subjects. He also wanted to reinforce his rule by calling on the assistance of the Almighty, and to make a link with the Byzantine empire, then the world power.

The story goes that in choosing a religion the prince summoned representatives of various faiths to visit his court in order, like carpet salesmen, to unroll their wares for his inspection. In a humorous nod to a Russian predilection the legend says that Vladimir rejected Islam because of its strictures against drinking, saying that this was the Russians' joy. At that time their drink was not vodka: this did not arrive in Russia, from Poland, until the sixteenth century.

The Eastern, or Greek, Orthodox religion won the contract because of the beauty of its church decoration and the magnificence of its liturgy, which together made congregations feel they were in heaven's ante-room. Doctrine, architecture, rituals and music – Russians embraced them all with enthusiasm and churches were raised in a frenzy of building. The characteristic domes, symbolising God, Christ and the apostles, were fashioned over the years into the quintessentially Russian onion shape that became a beloved feature of the landscape and of paintings, a comforting sentry-silhouette on every horizon.

The people filled their churches with icons, exquisite paintings of saints that remained for centuries the chief Russian art form. Dazzling splendour and jewel-box colour were a solace in famine, winter and oppression; so were rituals of worship, often rooted in pagan beliefs, which were part of the rhythm of the seasons and of the land. Ritual was always far more significant than theology. The church's authoritarian structure and dogmatic creed, its encourage-

ment of the acceptance of suffering and of autocratic rule, helped to
shape the Russian psyche.

Lenin, to whom religion was 'utterly vile', demanded in founding
his atheist state that 'reactionary clergy should be suppressed with
such cruelty that they will remember it for decades'. During his rule
hundreds of churches were destroyed and more than half the
monasteries closed. Church leaders bowed to the Soviet state,
hoping that the faith would somehow survive the storm. In the 1930s
Stalin directed a campaign of unparalleled ferocity. Tens of
thousands of priests were murdered and driven to exile and
thousands of churches were smashed and closed. Stalin ordered the
dynamiting of the Saviour's Cathedral in central Moscow, one of the
most magnificent Russian buildings ever raised. In its place he
ordered the construction of a great skyscraper that would be a
cathedral of the new order, awesome evidence of communist
achievement. But the engineers and architects, defeated by the
swampy ground, were unable to match the skills of the nineteenth-
century builders who had patiently raised the cathedral as a work of
thanksgiving for Russia's deliverance from Napoleon. The hole that
remained after the dynamiting was eventually made into an open-air
swimming pool. The water is warmed for all-season use and the
vapour drifts in clouds to a nearby art gallery and slowly eats at the
treasures within: Stalin's breath, an appropriately malignant legacy.

The churches that survived destruction were reminders of a faith
more ancient and enduring. Their domes were beacons gleaming in
a dark sea. People kept their traditions alive during the decades of
repression, taking risks to join in the rituals. Some had their
children baptised. At her home in a village in southern Russia
Gorbachev's mother took her son to the font.

Stalin hounded the church to the edge of extinction: Hitler
inadvertently played a part in saving it. Stalin needed all the help he
could get when the Germans rushed in and overwhelmed the Soviet
army. The Germans took advantage of his military weakness, seized
a huge stretch of territory, surrounded Leningrad and came within
sight of the domes of the Kremlin. The cornered Stalin permitted a
revival of the church to help reinforce a Russian nationalist spirit,
and priests were instructed to bless soldiers as they set off to fight for
motherland and Holy Russia. They prayed for Stalin, too. For the

church the war years were a reprieve, a vital breathing space. When Khrushchev came to power he vowed to complete Lenin's work and annihilate religion. In five years he closed many of the surviving churches and imposed severe limits on religious activity. This hostility continued in Brezhnev's time and his successor, Andropov, brought in more restrictions.

In the last two centuries of Tsarist rule the Orthodox Church was effectively a department of state; and so it was under the communists. The spiritual authority of its leaders was thereby undermined. The church's business was controlled by the Communist Party through the Council for Religious Affairs, with the KGB ever-attentive, ensuring that bishops and clergy were carefully watched and that, in the main, only compliant men rose to seniority. Licensed by the party, with its leaders at the Kremlin's bidding, the church was called on to support Soviet foreign policy, to be part of Moscow's veneer. It survived the communist tyranny, but brittle and much weakened, subservient, humiliated and reduced. Before the Revolution there were more than 54,000 churches. Seven thousand survived the communist onslaught. In the Soviet empire the church was to a large extent a fugitive and the faith lived like a flickering candle shielded from the wind by cupped hands.

In the late 1980s the Kremlin moderated its old hostility and permitted celebration of the thousandth anniversary of Russia's embracing of the Christian faith that had helped to shape it. The word 'God' had its capital letter officially restored. Gorbachev wanted more popular support, and antagonism to religion did not fit the image of a civilised society that the Soviet Union was trying to project abroad. There was also a need for a moral force in a demoralised country. Restrictions on the importing of bibles were relaxed and the Pope's Christmas message was broadcast for the first time on Soviet television. With the Gorbachev thaw people swarmed to be baptised. A priest remarked that he felt like a squeezed lemon after baptising crowds of a hundred at a time.

In the small hours of Easter Day, in the Cathedral of the Epiphany in Moscow, I found myself moulded like putty, trying to avoid having my eyebrows singed, as people crammed in, their hands around the dancing flames of their candles. The celebration of Easter morning is the most important service of the year and most of the congregation had arrived long before midnight, pushing and shouldering relentlessly through the door like commuters in the metro. The pungent smell of hundreds of candles made nostrils prickle. There are no pews in Russian churches, it being considered disrespectful to sit, and none of the formality of services in the West. People move about or stand, as they wish, and push and shove, too, as they do in the streets and shops. Here in the cathedral we were a herd, pushed inexorably, sometimes amiably, sometimes roughly, towards the cathedral's glory, the tall screen of icons. The scene was rich theatre, a gorgeous living tapestry, priests chanting prayers and the choir singing soaring phrases while crowned full-bearded bishops in brocades, silks and golden robes presided in shimmering splendour over the restless moving mass, the smell of sweat and oniony breath mingling with the incense and the vapour of melting wax.

Outside, a large force of police controlled the crowds and traffic, twirling black-and-white sticks. They were helped by police aux-iliaries, pasty-faced men with dull insolent eyes, like pub louts. Their duties had changed. It was not so long ago that the police and their unpleasant friends were sent to harass church-goers and to intimidate young believers. The authorities used to say scornfully that the church was supported only by a tribe of icon-kissing old women, and they put rock music on radio and television in a crude attempt to lure young people from the Easter services.

In the past few years, as church congregations have gathered strength, hardline atheism has everywhere receded. In Leningrad evening classes for atheists were cancelled for lack of interest, and in some schools in Moscow priests were invited to join discussions with students. The Easter service I attended was shown on television. In the chronicle of astonishments Gorbachev met the Pope, the first visit of a Kremlin boss to the Vatican. The wounded Russian church emerged from its imprisonment and subservience to seek its role and find a new relevance after the years of persecution.

★   ★   ★

From Byzantium the Russians took their Christian faith, the double-headed eagle of the Byzantine emperors which they made a Tsarist emblem, and their system of names. Many of these are of Greek origin and are part of a patronymic system that bestows three names on an individual: his Christian name, his father's name and his family name. Hence Mikhail Sergeyevich Gorbachev, Mikhail son of Sergei, politely addressed as Mikhail Sergeyevich. Lenin was – and still is – referred to respectfully as Vladimir Ilyich.

Gorbachev's family name is derived from a nickname or descriptive name meaning hunchback, just as Ryzhkov means red-haired, Kosygin means squint-eyed and Smirnoff means quiet. Many family names are occupational descriptions: Rybakov, a fisherman; Kalashnikov, a baker; Kuznetsov, a smith; Sereznikov, an earring-maker; Popov, a priest; Razpopov, an unfrocked priest. With a name that means thunder, General Gromov, who commanded Soviet forces in Afghanistan, seemed destined to be a soldier. Some of the British adventurers and merchants who settled in Russia left their names: Butler became Butlerov and Learmont, Lermontev.

Revolutionaries often hid behind pseudonyms to evade the secret police and also, perhaps, to reinvent themselves in the revolutionary life with its melodrama, invisible inks and false beards. Many of those who led the 1917 coup had assumed names: Lenin, Trotsky, Stalin, Zinoviev and Molotov. Vladimir Ilyich Ulyanov contrived the name Lenin from the Lena river, one of Russia's longest. It stretches through Siberia where he served a comfortable term of exile, hunting, shooting and fishing, swimming and ice-skating, reading and writing and, eventually, marrying the devoted Nadezhda Krupskaya. The only cloud in his idyll was the presence of his mother-in-law, whom he did not like: hence his remark that the punishment for bigamy is two mothers-in-law. Trotsky, Lev Davidovich Bronstein, took from a village the revolutionary name he used for his escape from Siberia. Stalin relished the name that meant steel, and liked to be called nothing else. It fitted the strong idea he had of himself, rather than the squat and shabby reality. In middle age he liked to see photographs of himself as a young man, when he had cut a dashing figure. As a revolutionary robbing banks for the Bolsheviks he had employed the name of Koba, a legendary outlaw in his native Georgia, and had already set aside his real name of Djugashvili, a name of Ossetian origin which means dross.

★   ★   ★

Before he set Russia on its Christian course Prince Vladimir of Kiev first attempted to invent a religion of his own to satisfy and unite his people and strengthen his rule. He erected idols of pagan gods and instructed people to worship them. This, however, was not success-ful and the prince began the search for a more convincing faith which culminated in him embracing the Orthodox religion. After the communists seized power they, too, found it necessary to invent a religion. This was partly to fill the space left by a Christianity retreating before the virulently atheist regime; but, more important-ly, it was to give the communists legitimacy and focus and provide a consolidating force. Lenin was the natural candidate for deification. Even before his death he was enshrined in the Bolshevik hagiogra-phy as a super-being. There were syrupy poems idealising him as a prophet, a knight in armour, a genius, a saint, a version of Christ. Verses began 'Hail to you' and heaped glory on his name. Books about him presented 'improved' accounts of his life, and his fiftieth birthday was the occasion for an outpouring of paeans which helped to make him a legend, a Messiah in a three-piece suit. The habit began of invoking Lenin's name in writings and speeches. Citing Lenin, Communists affirmed their allegiance to the cause.

When he died, Lenin provided his followers with a ready-made god, faith and icon to give the regime the legitimacy it craved and to provide a bridge from the Revolution into the future. His lying-in-state and funeral, attended by hundreds of thousands of people, persuaded the new leadership that although Lenin was dead, he could never be buried. (As for his being dead, stories persisted for years that he was really alive.) Lenin's widow famously implored the party not to let their 'sorrow for Ilyich find expression in outward veneration of his personality. Do not raise monuments to him or palaces to his name.'

But Stalin and the others had already decided that the 'great helmsman' did not belong to her. He was to serve the party as a mythological figure and was to be given a kind of immortality; his body was not to moulder but would remain whole, like the body of a saint. Denied a decent mortal exit, he would lie in pharaonic state, a sacred souvenir, filling a religious role and purpose. Lenin lives, went the slogan, and Stalin and his colleagues made sure that Father Lenin would continue to exist and that his tomb would be a shrine and a place of pilgrimage.

The body was put in the care of the Commission for the Immortalisation of the Memory of V. I. Ulyanov. Since it was showing signs of deterioration after the initial embalming, scientists and doctors were put to work at once to perfect, at high speed, a formula to preserve it. In a macabre drama they worked around the clock, experimenting on other bodies in the search for the right mixture. Their success was hailed as a feat of Soviet science, a communist triumph.

Illuminated like a jewel on a velvet cushion, the body was placed in its sepulchre in Red Square and committed to its posthumous existence. The red granite ziggurat of the tomb, which replaced the temporary wooden one, was the physical core of the Lenin cult and was built as a tribune, a royal box, as if the body, communism's amulet, would magically bestow strength and validity on those standing there. For Stalin it became a launching pad for his own personality cult.

The casting of Lenin statues became an industry in its own right. The man described by his admirer John Reed as having 'a short stocky figure with a big head, balding, and bulging, snubbish nose, little winking eyes' became one of the most sculpted and painted in the history of portraiture. A man's body clad in a suit must be a tedious subject for a sculptor, but the artists did their best. The men who made Lenin statues had their own union. Out of the studios and foundries came Lenins in their hundreds, usually giant-size, striding, declaiming, urging, coat tails flying to suggest the energy of the man, waistcoat bared. The head became more stylised, often more emblem than portrait, the dome suggesting power, eyes set in a condor's glare, Tartar features muted or emphasised to taste, beard thrust forward like a cutwater. (Lenin did not have a beard during the days of the Revolution: he shaved it off because he was in hiding from the authorities; and he wore a wig to complete the disguise.)

There were Lenins for all seasons: on coins, banknotes, stamps, lamps, paperweights, tapestries, mosaics, carpets, stained-glass windows, in huge portraits made of flowers. There was Lenin stern, Lenin grim, Lenin wry, Lenin thoughtful, Lenin as avuncular as Colonel Sanders. His image fulfilled the incantation that 'Lenin is always with us'.

After the three Baltic republics were seized under the robbers' pact made by Stalin and Hitler, black statues of Lenin were placed in their capitals, like giant chess pieces thumped down to mark possession of territory.

Every city had its Lenin square and Lenin avenue, Lenin factory and Lenin library; and every rural district its Lenin farm. Forty cities were given his name and the second highest mountain in the country, in the Pamirs, was renamed Mount Lenin, the highest being Mount Communism. Lenin corners, communist shrines, were set up in factories. In private homes, too, space was set aside to honour the dictator.

No public place, no civil service corridor lacked its portrait of Lenin. Every party official's office I visited seemed to be the same: the portrait of Lenin, the pristine collected works of more than fifty volumes, the clear desk with its telephone and pen set, and no sign of work being done.

The tomb in Red Square was the central part of the jigsaw. It was guarded by KGB troops who looked particularly sharp and clean. The sentries changed every hour with an immaculate drill performed to the striking of the clock on the Saviour's Tower, the Kremlin's Big Ben. It was like a sinister ballet, performed by clockwork soldiers, legs encased in polished black boots kicking out robotically, arms swinging in slow rhythm across the chest. When I joined the long queue for the tomb one day I found myself under the beady scrutiny of the guards who kept the line in order. One of them jabbed my neighbour's arm. 'Hey you – button your jacket.' His eyes roved down the line and did not conceal distaste, as if he felt we were not worthy to enter the sanctum. He saw a woman with a cardigan over her arm. 'Hey you – put that on.' Men instinctively straightened their ties. 'You – get your hands out of your pockets.' There was a nervous anticipatory clearing of throats, and hats were removed. Voices which had been low and respectful fell away.

Another guard glared at us and raised a warning, silencing index finger to his lips.

Inspected, tidied, silenced, rebuked, intimidated, under the surveillance of many eyes, we passed like prisoners through the bronze doors, past the glittering bayonets of the rigid tight-mouthed sentries, and descended the porphyry staircase into the obsidian blackness of the tomb.

Once inside there was no time to pause or linger. We were kept moving through the vault, prodded here and there by guards. In the centre of the black and grey chamber the glass sarcophagus lay raised upon a black catafalque. A KGB sentry stood at each corner, motionless and taut, with rifle and bayonet, reminding me of the soldiers who stand at the lying-in-state of kings.

There was an undoubted tension, a sense of breath being held. No one dared even whisper. In the gloom of the crypt the concentrated pool of light in the centre was dramatically bright and white, lending a luminous quality to the face and hands of the corpse. The aspect of the head and countenance was familiar, the pilgarlic dome, high cheekbones and small fox-red beard and moustache. The waxy face wore to my mind the faintest of frowns, though to others the expression has appeared an inscrutable smile. It was odd to think that this man, when he lived in London, could be seen popping out to the shops for bread and a bottle of red wine. The corpse was dressed in a black jacket and a blue tie with white spots, neat and conservative; but from the chest downwards it was enveloped in black draperies which conveyed a suggestion of incompleteness.

The line wound around three sides of the sarcophagus and did not stop. There was no moment to stand and stare. Near the exit was a guard whose main function, it seemed, was to catch the elbows of those who, taking a final backward glance, stumbled on the steps.

Although glimpsed only fleetingly, the black-and-white starkness and bizarre theatricality of the spectacle lodged it permanently in the memory, as if a shutter had exposed imperishable film. The purpose of this place was to awe. It was the heart of things – not so much the heart of the faith, more the heart of the deception – the node of the cult through which the communist leaders reinforced their claim to rule. The corpse was their talisman and ju-ju, as cosseted as an idol in a temple. Over the years its servants maintained it, its tailors stitched its suits and chose its neckties. Perhaps agents shopped abroad for it. When the Germans were marching on Moscow the body was removed and taken like a treasure in a specially-equipped railway car to a hiding place in Kuibyshev, in the Ural mountains. The German high-water mark was ten miles from the tomb.

Stalin, after his death in 1953, lay for eight years alongside Lenin, a grisly bedfellow. Lenin, a man of a certain rectitude who would have deplored his own enshrinement, would surely have been doubly appalled that a man he regarded as rude and dubious should be lodged alongside him. Then history was rewritten, and the cuckoo in the crypt was moved out and buried in the Kremlin wall. Lenin was again alone.

In the two minutes I was in the tomb a storm broke over Red Square and heavy rain hosed the people waiting to get in. But no one ran for cover. People stood, drenched and stoical. Having made the pilgrimage to Moscow and waited for hours, they were not to be deterred by a soaking. As I walked away a bride emerged from the tomb on the arm of her new husband, one hand clutching her hat, the other hoisting her billowing dress from the wet cobbles as she skittered on her expensive new high heels. It was a custom for newly-married couples to visit the mausoleum, as if to have their union blessed by the relic. To complete the ritual they walked from the square to place their flowers on the tomb of the Unknown Soldier beside the Kremlin wall.

Not all of Lenin was preserved in the mausoleum. His brain was removed to be pickled in paraffin forever as a priceless relic. It was the founding organ of the Institute of the Brain, established to discover if there were any connection between brain structure and genius. A Russian reporter interviewed the Institute's director about the research, still secret work, and asked: 'What can be said about politicians after the study of their brains?' The director answered: 'Nothing, so far.'

Other brains subsequently joined the collection. Among them were those of the scientist Ivan Pavlov, of conditioned reflexes and dog fame, the poet Vladimir Mayakovsky, and the writer Maxim Gorky, apologist for the Stalin regime and the secret police. There is also the brain of Sergei Kirov, the Leningrad party chief murdered on Stalin's orders, whose killing Stalin used as the excuse for the horrific purge in which millions were slaughtered. Stalin's brain is also in a jar in this strange repository.

Lenin spent his last years in a country house twenty-one miles from Moscow at Gorki Leninskiye, a handsome nineteenth-century white and ochre mansion, once the home of a mayor of Moscow, standing amid birches and conifers. As the place of Lenin's death, it is another carefully-kept shrine. Visitors must wear large slippers over their shoes so that their feet look like those of Mickey Mouse. When I went, the first stop was the telephone room where the frustrated Lenin used to shout down the line to the Kremlin. The instrument was his despair, and he wrote to the telephone manager saying that the engineers who had been sent to repair the instrument were either 'complete fools or clever saboteurs'. The letter apparently had little effect, and Lenin penned another note threatening the wretched phone-men with execution.

The hunting jacket Lenin wore in the woods hereabouts was displayed in a case. The guide briskly recited the appropriate statistics: jacket size 50, boots size 39, Lenin 167 centimetres tall. (At 5 ft 5 in he was an inch taller than Stalin; even so, his feet did not touch the floor as he sat in his office chair in the Kremlin.)

His cinema-projector was in the drawing room. In the hall was the shiny black electric wheelchair presented to him by British workers in 1923, the year before he died. Lenin never used it. All the clocks in the house were stopped at 6.50, the time of his death on the evening of 21 January, and all the lamps were covered with black cloth. On the table of the room where he died was the December 1923 edition of the journal of the British Communist Party and works by Maxim Gorky and Jack London, whose adventure stories were read to Lenin as he lay dying. In the garage I was shown Lenin's Rolls-Royce, fitted out for winter driving with a caterpillar track at the back and skis at the front. As I left the guide anticipated my question and, as if daring me to disagree, said: 'The interest in Lenin is as great as ever. The fact is that Lenin is the only politician whose authority is still indisputable.'

Only after I had left the house did it occur to me that I had seen no portrait of Lenin there. It must have been the only public building in Russia which lacked one. There were hundreds of portraits, however, in the Lenin Museum overlooking Red Square. In thirty-four rooms of Leniniana were displayed the chairs he sat in, the clothes he wore and the jacket with holes in it said to have been made by the bullets fired by his would-be assassin Fanny Kaplan in 1918. There was also his death mask. The museum's purpose was Leninolatry and the glorification of Soviet rule, and its selection of material made it like a huge version of the Soviet photographs altered by propagandists to remove the images of men who fell from favour. Stalin was edited-out after he was condemned by Khrushchev, just as his statues were removed from town squares. There was not much of Trotsky to be seen, either, although there would not have been much of a revolution without him. But he had been cast in the role of devil to Lenin's god and Stalin's prophet.

I asked the museum director about this, and she agreed that much had been hidden away but said that in the current atmosphere of greater openness records were being taken from the vaults and put on display to give a more accurate impression of Soviet history. A number of faked photographs were being replaced by originals, and some former non-persons were being released from their photographic exile. One of the new exhibits she showed me was a huge painting by Isaak Brodsky, the party's court painter, of the Communist Congress of 1920. It depicts the complete cast of 340 characters and it had lain rolled up for decades, too full and truthful a picture for display. As for showing pictures of Stalin, the director said carefully that 'there are complications . . . we don't want to make an icon of anyone, but we do not want blank spots either.'

A friend said:

Imagine how bewildering it is for us Russians. Our history is constantly starting, stopping and restarting. It has been rewritten, hidden and forbidden, then suddenly permitted. Whole decades have disappeared from the history books and important individuals have been wiped from our memory. The story of our own existence is protected by taboos. Scholars are paid to write lies and historians are trained to conceal. In the West you have reassessment and revision as new information becomes available – that is natural. But we have total obliteration. It is as if we are hypnotised from time to time and told: It didn't happen.

When Stalin was alive we had a version of history in which he was the greatest man in the world and we were told to revere him as a god. After he died history began again. There was a clean slate. The statues were torn down and the books rewritten. When Khrushchev was deposed it was as if he had never been. When Brezhnev died our memories had to be corrected. We were told that his eighteen years were the years of stagnation.

When Gorbachev arrived in 1985 history started all over again and we were permitted to read this and remember that. We were suddenly allowed greater access to our own national memory. What we found out naturally came as a great shock to many of us. So many skeletons in the cupboards. We gained a better idea of how our minds were manipulated and how much had been hidden, how much we had been lied to. We learnt, for example, of the extent of the brutality of the state. But many people said it was wrong to expose these things, to dwell on the mistakes of the past.

In 1990 it was officially admitted that school history books were travesties, and history examinations throughout the country were suspended for a year while new books were written.

In the Lenin Museum my eye was caught by three large illuminated scrolls. These were the petitions by which Estonia, Latvia and Lithuania supposedly asked to be admitted to the Soviet Union in 1940. They did not ask to join: they were the spoils of war, and these scrolls dressed up the fraud with fine calligraphy. In this and other ways the museum held up a mirror to the Soviet state's dishonesties.

Communists were shocked in 1990 when one of the new liberal politicians suggested that Lenin should be decently buried. It was considered a blasphemy, but the fact that he said it openly was another sign of communism's failing authority. The mausoleum lay at the heart of the cult which, with its claims of Soviet success and superiority, was part of that larger lie to which the threadbare Soviet reality bore witness. The statues picketing the land pointed to nowhere. The tomb stood as an obstacle to a proper confrontation with truth.

★   ★   ★

After the tanks and troops had gone from Red Square, Gorbachev broke with tradition and walked across the cobbles at the head of a procession of Muscovites. He walked beside Boris Yeltsin, the central figure of the alternative politics which took root in the Gorbachev era as communism's authority and credibility retreated. Like Gorbachev, Yeltsin had spent his life inside the party machine, and like Gorbachev he had once believed that communism could be reformed and modernised. The essential difference was that he realised after a while that this was impossible, that communism was not susceptible to political alchemy. He therefore struck out on a new road, repudiated communism and attracted enormous support as a politician of conviction and honesty. The party hounded him and the hardliners hated him. Their enmity made him even more popular. His position was secured when, in Russia's first democratic elections, he became leader of the Russian republic. He quit the Communist Party in a dramatic, televised episode, and set out to free Russia completely from the party that had ruled it so disastrously.

So the Revolution Day parade concluded. Gorbachev did not see the march that followed, the procession of tens of thousands of supporters of radical groups bearing banners calling the 1917 Revolution a tragedy. Down with the Communist Party, they shouted, down with Lenin. An old man of eighty-six, watching all this from the sidelines, buttonholed me and said: 'I've seen everything now. When I was a boy I saw Lenin walk across this very square after the Revolution. Then they loved him. Now they hate him. It has come full circle. I never thought I'd see it.'

The authorities posted a strong force of toughs, mostly wearing the woollen ski caps that seemed to be standard KGB wardrobe issue, to form a wall around Lenin's tomb. But the marchers were peaceful enough and the guards had only to put up with the rebuking fingers of middle-aged women who told them: 'You ought to be ashamed of yourselves.'

A large gang of men strode across the square as the demonstration petered out. They sniggered and said 'Watch out – we're the Black Hundred' – the name of the Russian nationalist fanatics of the early part of the century who carried out pogroms against students and Jews. The crude joke was a reminder that anti-Semitism and the hunting of other traditional scapegoats was increasing as the country's troubles grew.

Suddenly, the square was deserted. For a few minutes the pigeons had it to themselves and leaves and pieces of paper swirled about in a gust of wind. A group of women arrived, short and plump and sturdy with round weatherbeaten faces, red noses and large rough hands. They wore headscarves and boots and wielded country brooms made of twigs. These were the charladies of Red Square. They bent their backs like gleaners and moved slowly over the cobbles, picking up history's litter, sweeping clean the heart of Russia.

2

SAM' SQUARE

A Russian smell was already lodged in my memory before I first arrived in the chocolate gloom of Sheremetyevo airport. As a boy I visited the cruisers which brought Khrushchev and Bulganin to Portsmouth. The sailors gave us red enamel badges with the hammer and sickle insignia and also pungent cigarettes which we smoked clandestinely until we felt queasy and our jackets reeked of Russia. It was a component of all the country's smells, of the cabbagy garlicky staleness of crowded airless places, the mossy *pissoir* odour in tenement stairwells, the stench of squalid beerhalls. It mingled with the sharp whiff of kebab stalls in the parks and the stink of low-grade petrol in the streets.

Before I went to the Soviet Union many of the images I had of it hung on words invested with a chill or brooding resonance: gulag, Lubyanka, KGB, Stalin, Lenin. Soviet itself meant something bleak. Kremlin suggested labyrinths and omerta. The syllables of 'Moscow' spoke of drama and power and in my imagination it was a place of newsreel grey. But at its heart, inside its concrete palisades of dreary tower blocks, it is a yellow city, butterscotch and ochre, primrose and cream, varied by Nile green and pink and oxblood red. The jagged cardiogram pinnacles of the gigantic Stalin towers, whose sunset silhouettes lend a shivery drama to the city skyline, proclaim power and pomposity. But many parts of Moscow are on a human scale and the old quarters are still beautiful, particularly under the brilliant blue of winter morning skies, the slanting light, and the merciful bandaging of snow. There are still wooden buildings of the nineteenth century, bent and sagging, which survived the drive in the 1960s to get rid of them all and which stand, as they always did, in broken, muddy streets.

In a few years of walking around my own neighbourhood I developed an affection for the elegant mansions which had fallen on hard times. I saw the window-sills break and stucco flake as buildings became poor dowagers and walls bulged with paunches, as if suddenly uncorseted. People deserted them and a mildew smell issued from their sad, worn doorways. There was not the money, nor perhaps the will, to stop the dilapidation. The crumbling seemed all of a piece with the decay of a system which had overreached itself and could not keep up appearances.

Like most foreign correspondents in Moscow I lived in an apartment building set aside for journalists, diplomats and other foreigners. It was a solid beige nine-storey block built by German prisoners of the Second World War and stood on the ring road that follows the line of the city's sixteenth-century earthen fortifications. Because of its address in Sadovo Samotechnaya Street it was known as Sad Sam. There was only one entrance to our courtyard and it was monitored by policemen in a cramped sentry box. Although this seemed to have room for only one man, especially in winter when guards were fattened by sheepskin coats, there were often two men trying to squeeze in, sometimes a third.

In Gorbachev's period of relative relaxation it was easier for Soviet citizens to walk into the courtyard without being turned away by the police. In an earlier era Russian guests had to be met and escorted into flats; and then sometimes with difficulty. But there was no oppressive surveillance. I assumed there were listening devices in the flats and that the KGB could open the doors if it wanted. I assumed, too, that my telephone conversations were listened to from time to time, but the clicks no doubt sprang more from the vagaries of a third-rate telephone system than from eavesdropping. I never found a pretty girl in my hotel room, nor a plain one for that matter. I did not feel it necessary to take the precaution diplomats took, of travelling in company outside Moscow. I was once telephoned by a man who said he had important documents to show me and suggested a rendezvous under the clock of the puppet theatre across the ring road, but this seemed too crudely melodramatic to be a real provocation. I told him I was too busy. Once, when I was dining with another reporter in a hotel restaurant in Moscow, a man appeared suddenly and sat down with us. Announcing that he was 'a typical Russian engineer' on business in the city, he began to engage us in conversation. I was certain he was in the KGB because, in a restaurant where the service was notably slow, his meal, and his

Georgian wine, arrived almost as soon as he had sat down. The KGB, too, marched on its stomach.

Of course, our movements were monitored and restricted. Foreigners' cars have distinctive yellow number-plates; they are also distinctively foreign, mostly Volvos. We moved freely within the Moscow city limits but had to notify the foreign ministry of our plans to travel outside. Depending on the destination we had to give twenty-four or forty-eight hours' notice, and permission could be refused because of political trouble. Some places were closed to us from time to time: Armenia, Azerbaijan, Georgia and Lithuania, for example. On one occasion I asked for permission to go to the hat market at Khimki on the outskirts of Moscow and was refused. Soviet reporters in parts of the West were under similar excessive restrictions. The KGB kept track of foreigners on the move through its web of informants in hotels and other places. Intourist guides used to report on every tourist and businessman they escorted, adding to the KGB's mass of useless information. When I asked a former Intourist guide in Lithuania about it, she said she had not reported on a foreigner for years. 'Soviet work, not Lithuanian,' she said.

Our apartment was large and comfortable with high ceilings and big windows, much more spacious than the average Russian dwelling. The foreigners' flats in Moscow, like the homes of expatriates anywhere, usually exhibited local art and ornament. There would be Russian paintings, an engraving of an old church with its napiform domes, a bazaar-bargained carpet or two from Central Asia, a Brezhnev moneybox doll, some Russian nesting dolls – perhaps one or two dolls too many – taking their places alongside artefacts from other foreign sojourns: Mexican puppets, Hindu idols, Zulu masks, jade Buddhas and Amazonian fertility symbols.

The furniture was foreign, usually Scandinavian, for Soviet furniture was in short supply. Russians remain for years on waiting lists for beds, sofas and kitchen equipment, and state furniture showrooms have large signs, like scoreboards, showing how long people have to wait for the goods they order. In one store I visited the scoreboard showed 1,500 people waiting for a popular bedroom suite, made in Eastern Europe, and the flinty-faced administrator said with just a dash of relish that this meant a wait of up to two years. People buy through their factory or trade union organisation and there is no hire-purchase. In an electrical appliance shop nearby the wait for a refrigerator was one year and a notice said that priority would be given to war veterans and widows. It is useful to know and cultivate such people. A long line waited to buy electric irons and some people were buying two or three. 'We might not see them again for years,' a man said.

When I went to Moscow I took with me a mosquito net and cockroach powder, to defend myself against the city's chief pests. Sad Sam had plenty of cats to deal with the mice. Cockroaches, with their Stalin-whiskered faces, infest all old buildings and are no respecters of caste; there is a strong contingent at the British Embassy, one of Moscow's most handsome buildings and once the home of a sugar magnate. The other curse of Sad Sam was the thunder of traffic on the ring road far into the night. People who knew Moscow thirty years ago remember traffic so light that the broad avenues looked like deserted runways at an airport. Russians said the high volume of late traffic was caused by people visiting friends and restaurants, driving to and from factories, plying for hire to boost their income in a city where there are not enough licensed cabs, driving around to find relief from desperately overcrowded flats, and, similarly, taking their girlfriends for a drive because a car is one of the few places where privacy can be found.

★   ★   ★

To get a breath of Moscow's polluted air I would often walk from our block along Yermolova Street. Sometimes I went through the scruffy entrance of Bakery No. 675 to buy a loaf for a few kopecks. Following the example of canny women shoppers, I tested the bread for freshness by squeezing it with the metal spatula provided.

Early one morning I walked around the corner from the bakery to attend the Day of Knowledge at School No. 30. This was the first day of September, the traditional start to the school year, and Russians always make an occasion of it. By 7.30 the playground was filling up with parents, grandparents and pupils, and an apprehensive tribe of Natashas and Sashas starting school at the age of seven after attending kindergarten. They were a picture in their new uniforms. The girls wore black dresses, white pinafores and white stockings and had white ribbons in their shining hair, a school costume dating back to the nineteenth century. The boys wore dark blue tunics and long trousers and all the pupils had new satchels on their backs and carried flowers for their teachers. Many of the mothers were dressed in their best clothes, grandmothers fussed over the little girls' hair ribbons and fathers took snapshots.

A six-piece band, the musicians wearing bow-ties and playing trumpets and cornets, filled the air with cheerful tunes. The school banners, red with yellow fringes, were paraded by Young Pioneers, fledgling members of the communist youth organisation, wearing red scarves around their necks, while the band played the national anthem in salute. One of the new girls was hoisted onto the shoulders of a senior boy and carried around the playground, ringing a bell to signal the start of lessons. The children formed up and marched towards the school door and several mothers ran forward to give a squeeze around the shoulders, a final kiss on the cheek. 'Be a good girl, be a good boy.' Then the playground was suddenly empty and the trumpets died away. For a while a knot of parents stared at the school door. Tears glistened in mothers' eyes, grandmothers sniffled and fathers blinked hard. They reluctantly tore themselves away.

On the other side of the street, opposite the bakery, was the house where Vladimir Vysotsky once lived. It usually had a group of Russian tourists outside and a bunch of flowers attached to the door. Vysotsky was a people's hero, a rebel minstrel in the Bob Dylan mould, who wrote and sang in his gravelly way of the cruelties and banalities of Soviet tyranny. Amateur tape recordings of his songs were part of the currency of underground culture and his records, now on open sale, remain immensely popular. Self-destructive and romantic, Vysotsky died of drink at forty-two.

The road turned past shabby houses ripe for demolition, past a garment factory, past a tall yellow house with a frieze of vampires, past an art school where the students at their easels always seemed to be drawing the same plaster bust. I would cross the road to the Hermitage gardens and walk among the trees where grandmothers and grandfathers wheeled papooses in prams and lovers flung themselves into sudden, careless, astonishing clinches. There was a muffled *pfft-pfft* from the indoor air-rifle range, and in fine weather the *click-clack* of chess pieces moved in the high-speed games conducted under a drifting cloud of smoke from intently-drawn cigarettes. In small pavilions, little rustic readeries, people would pass the afternoon hours at anchor in their books, as peaceful as a painting.

Sometimes I turned right out of our block, towards Samotechnaya Square and the new metro station. It had recently been opened, an addition to a system famous for cheapness, cleanliness and efficiency: five kopecks for an unlimited journey and a very frequent service. The decoration of this station was modest compared with the gorgeous metro temples of the Stalin era. Whenever a new station was opened in those days, crowds gathered to marvel at vaulted gold ceilings, mosaics, stained glass and sculptures. As the cathedrals of faith were being torn down on the surface, these cathedrals of transport were being built far below. Down the slope, on the way to the station, stood an elderly crooked wooden house with carved windows, a piece of the village come to town, leaning so heavily on its history that I feared my own footfall would bring it crashing down. On the pavement a man sold apples from crates, mean little green apples, each looking as if it had been individually bruised by a hammer.

There was always a queue at the video parlour. It showed old foreign films, motel rejects, Rambo adventures and scratchy stuff with glimpses of naked women, the soundtracks dubbed in a monotone with no distinction between male and female voices. Video parlours were the new entertainment. Some of the operators, in whom the spirit of prude and censor was strong, would switch the video machine to fast-forward when sex scenes started, giving Russians a curious notion of the nature of sexual intercourse in the West.

There was a crowd at the door of the sausage café because the sausages were better than average and there was a rank and watery beer to be had. Sausage is such a staple that cartoonists use it to represent food in general. It is often smelly and fatty. Not long ago a newspaper reported that most cats, when offered state-made sausage, walked away from it. Readers wrote in to say that they had tried the cat test, with the same result.

A knick-knack kiosk had such a motley selection of things for sale – combs, badges, key-rings – that it seemed the owner had emptied a silted-up drawer onto the counter. The ice-cream shop was full: ice-cream is the chief fast food of the country, and the queues are as long in winter as in summer. People eat two or three at once. Russians love ice-cream so much that if the supply stopped there would be riots. Similarly, there was a large congregation at the tobacco kiosk. Russians smoke a lot and when cigarette production broke down the government had to rush in supplies from Eastern Europe. Foreign cigarettes became an alternative currency. When I wanted a taxi in the street I would hold up my hand and display a packet of Marlboro. In a few seconds a driver would see the red and white packet and forge through the traffic like a shark scenting blood.

On the corner of the street was a derelict building covered with torn posters and graffiti and a wall filled with handwritten advertisements, mostly appeals for apartments or for flats for exchange. Such spaces perform the function of the small-ads sections of Western newspapers. A policeman guarded the door of the liquor shop. Queues formed two hours before it opened at 2 p.m. Men with grey, quarried faces crept forward like a chain gang. Other faces were stamped with anger and humiliation. Liquor queues were often unruly, people pushing their way forward and others trying to wheedle their way in. A scrum often formed around the entrance. Red-eyed drunks hung around hopelessly, poorly dressed and slate-blue with cold. Other men roamed up and down looking for like-minded souls who would share the cost of a bottle of vodka or cheap wine. A few old people earned a rouble or two by queuing on behalf of others. Women endured the humiliations and roughness of this worst of queues to buy wine and sweet Russian champagne for a wedding or birthday feast, an act of love and devotion. Russians will suffer days of thin commons to pay for royal extravagance.

Drink, the Russian love for it, is a subject in which debate about tradition becomes entangled with argument about the effects of the communist assault on the people. Alcoholism is widespread and, as it is anywhere else, a cause of much crime, absenteeism and divorce;

it is doubtless one reason why the expectation of life among men is falling. The capacity for strong drink and the boisterousness of feasts has been marvelled at by travellers and celebrated by poets down the centuries. Russians hold that vodka is sunshine for the soul, a comfort in dark tedious winters, and that since God made them drinkers there is nothing they can do but accept their fate. Some argue that a people who were traditionally exuberant drinkers, who enjoyed their binges, were pushed to desperate and depressed drinking by a communist regime that robbed them of humanity.

> We were always drinkers, Soviet life made us drunks [a friend said]. We are disillusioned. We have been given nothing to believe in. Communism made cynics of us all. There are many in middle age who started out with an idealistic belief in communism. Imagine how they feel when they realise that everything they worked for is a lie and a ruin. They realise that their lives have been wasted and so they suffer spiritual collapse. It dawns on them that they have been victims in a huge experiment which has lasted for most of the twentieth century, that everything was a failure and a mistake.

Moscow had a famous tavern life in pre-revolutionary times but most of the beer houses were swept away in the puritanical and ideological fervour of the 1920s and 1930s when priggish young communist zealots sought to improve society. Today there are hardly any civilised and sociable places where Russians can drink. The only decent bars are in hotels for foreigners which, to most Russians, are forbidden cities where only foreign currency may be spent. Most pubs are stinking and disgusting, nightmarish swills like a Hogarth drawing, so crowded that men wait for hours to get in. The beer tastes foul and drinkers like to charge it up with vodka, the better to reach oblivion. Old hands bring empty milk cartons because there is always a shortage of glasses. Drunks stagger into the streets and are often run over. But the people are tolerant of their lurching wounded, and the police go around picking them up from the streets and taking them to drying-out 'tanks' as matter-of-factly as they might pick up litter.

Many women thought Gorbachev was right to launch his assault on drinking when he took power, for they are usually the victims of drink and drunken violence. But men saw the campaign which restricted liquor shop hours and the quantities that could be sold as another Kremlin assault made without much thought for the consequences. On top of other indignities, they said, the state made them queue for hours for the balm that gave them relief from oppression.

When Russians discuss the wretched aspects of their lives they list not only food shortages and crime but also *bezdushi*, heartlessness or soullessness, the erosion of compassion, dignity and decency. Newspapers comment that the Soviet Union has become 'de-civilised', that courtesy and neighbourliness have waned while indifference and selfishness are spreading.

It is hardly surprising [a woman said]. Since the Revolution our rulers have crushed decent feelings. They encouraged informers and made a virtue of lying. They ruled by fear and tried to destroy our culture. They saw no value in conscience – they laughed at it. We have become coarsened. We don't care about each other. You will hear people say that suffering has made us purer and somehow better, that if we don't have food at least we have soul. Go to the shops where there is nothing on the shelves and see how these purer people snarl at each other.

We are surly. Rudeness is such a normal part of life that we hardly think about it – the arrogance of bureaucrats exercising their bit of power, the bad manners of doctors, the sneering of the police.

Another woman agreed.

There used to be a stronger family and neighbourly feeling. You can't borrow a cup of sugar now. Maybe there is not so much sugar to give, but we have also become crueller and tougher. We don't have much sympathy for invalids. Old people who have no sons or daughters to help them are neglected. What an example for children: rudeness all around them. Is it any wonder? We spend our lives scrabbling for food and standing in queues. We live in overcrowded flats and you can't imagine the squabbling over shared kitchens and bathrooms. Seven or eight families sharing, just think of the potential for trouble. Young couples live with their in-laws and many have just a curtain for privacy. We have come to expect that people will be nasty, that nothing will be done without a bribe, so we are corrupt in a corrupted society, with no faith or direction. We feel ashamed.

Women bear the brunt of the callousness. Millions of them work in unpleasant jobs, spend hours hunting for food after work and somehow feed and clothe and bring up their children. Some women friends were amused when I asked them about a newspaper report of a young woman who had put a notice on one of the informal small-ads walls advertising 'Man for Sale'. A reporter telephoned the advertiser, who said she was renting out her husband for a hundred roubles a night and had built up a steady clientele. The women agreed: no Russian man is worth a hundred roubles a night. But suppose, they added, he is a good plumber, a skilled motor mechanic, or a genius who can resuscitate a broken-down black-market video machine; and suppose he is also hardworking, romantic and sober – *then* he could be a prince. Good men are hard to find, and many Russian women think men are lazy and too fond of drink. On the other hand, many of them are sympathetic and believe that communism has crushed initiative and creativity and the best masculine qualities. Mass death in war and in the camps deprived many women of their menfolk. Poor housing, drink and violence, separation and divorce – all these, too, have forced millions of women to be more dependent on themselves and on each other. Many women say that men have lost respect for them; but men have also lost respect for themselves.

★   ★   ★

Across the street men and women stood shoulder to shoulder reading the newspapers pinned up inside glass-fronted display cases. Absorbing the news was a serious and significant activity. Gorbachev allowed the press more freedom as a way of stimulating interest in reform; but whether he intended this openness to go as far as it did is hard to say. Given an inch, the small but significant group of radical newspapers gradually took a yard. The explosion of information was a phenomenon of the Gorbachev period that played a vital part in the political education of the people, in the growth of democratic politics and, ultimately, in the fall of communism.

Newspapers were in the front line of the struggle for the future of the Soviet Union. On one side was ranged the official press, tightly controlled, working loyally in the service of party and government, helping to organise 'the masses', as Soviet citizens were called. These newspapers had the bulk of the resources, the printing plants and the newsprint. On the other side were newspapers and writers with an urge to tell the truth to a population raised on lies and propaganda. It was a struggle, not for profit but for influence, a struggle for ideas. The circulation war was fought between old and new, past and future, hardliners and democrats. The old papers shrank like sandbanks before an encroaching sea as the new papers gained in confidence and authority.

Among the newspapers which broke new ground was *Argumenty i Fakty*. It became the paper with the largest circulation in the world, more than 33 million. The appetite for it was insatiable, and finding enough newsprint for it a perpetual battle. It was so popular that it could not be found on the news-stands. Every copy went to people who took out subscriptions to ensure that they received it. If you opened it on the street, a crowd gathered.

The newspaper was founded by Vladislav Starkov, an amiable, mild-mannered man, as a little news digest which he produced on his kitchen table. 'I started it', he said to me, 'because I did not trust the press. People ceased to believe the official newspapers years ago. They were fed up with being deceived.' He set out to meet the simple craving for unembroidered facts, for relief from propaganda, and produced an eight-page tabloid, a news concentrate without advertisements, its articles fresh, clear and short, without editorials, partisanship or ideology. Yury Sigov, one of the reporters, said 'the paper is popular because it is true.'

Until 1985 *Argumenty i Fakty* was, like all newspapers, under the control of the Communist Party ideology department. It obeyed party directives on what to publish. But with the onset of a policy of openness the grip of the apparatchiks weakened and the newspaper was no longer subordinate. The party hardliners waged their war mostly by trying to restrict supplies of newsprint: *Argumenty i Fakty*'s weekly digest of simple truths and revelations made the Soviet establishment grind its teeth. 'We live on a knife-edge,' Starkov said. 'Our hands shake when we sign to authorise printing. But if we didn't tremble a little we would be worried – we would feel we were not producing an interesting edition. Our lives as journalists were easier in Brezhnev's time because we knew exactly what we could and could not publish. Now we have to push the boundaries and see what happens. Facts, after all, can be subversive.'

Starkov had a famous collision with Gorbachev, who was infuriated by a report about reform and summoned editors to his office to haul them over the coals. 'Reading our newspapers,' he said, 'you would think the Soviet Union is a lake of petrol just waiting for a match.' Gorbachev demanded Starkov's resignation. Starkov stood his ground and refused. It was astonishing and unique: the man who said *No* to the power of the Kremlin. Starkov recalled: 'In the presence of everyone he asked me to retire, but I did not.' He shrugged. 'You can say that a complicated period of my life began. But life is impossible without struggle. In our society the conditions of the struggle have, fortunately, changed. The authorities don't hammer their fists on the table any more.'

Gorbachev was dealing with more than one brave editor. Starkov's staff said they would quit if he was removed; and readers rallied to his support. Had Gorbachev persisted with his demand for Starkov's head, he would have betrayed his own reforms. Starkov was protected to some extent by readers to whom *Argumenty i Fakty* was more than a newspaper. Like the other radical journals it represented hope, the possibility of the change they ached for. It was one of the few things they could trust.

★   ★   ★

As I turned the corner into the market the Caucasian flower sellers would beckon me over, primping the petals and leaves of their roses, tulips and carnations, always expensive but always sold because Russians love flowers and give them generously. Inside the market the vendors up from Azerbaijan and Georgia and Central Asia presided over mounds of melons, pomegranates, dried apricots, cherries, walnuts, apples and raisins while housewives pursed their lips and grumbled at the high prices. I would sometimes see the traders in the evening, in the restaurant up the road, ordering snowy mountains of rice pilaf and kebab, laughing uproariously over their brandy, linking arms and dancing to the rowdy band.

The market had its place in the tangled and rusted Soviet food chain. As a hall of plenty in a land of chronic shortages it was one of numerous paradoxes. The world shook its head at the spectacle of a country with vast farmlands producing huge harvests, yet forever on the edge of disaster, unable to feed its people properly. Ministers wrung their hands and warned of catastrophe next week or next month. Immense quantities of food rotted away. The army was sent to reap corn and dig potatoes, the authorities threatened and bullied people to help bring the harvest in; and still the shelves in the state shops were nearly empty and the queues grew longer and the world wondered whether there would be starvation.

This was, and is, unlikely. The Russian food problem is one of shortages and hardship rather than famine. People suffer malnutrition caused by poor diet, a lack of vitamins, bad meat, rotting potatoes and bruised fruit and vegetables. Cheese and sausage are scarce. Television programmes show orchards and fields bearing abundant crops, but the food never seems to reach the shops on time, if at all.

Except in the most fortunate areas of Russia, agriculture has always been hard and people have bent under the burden of winter. Much of the land is too far north for easy cultivation. The Soviet experiment, its vaunted agricultural revolution, has failed. Ideology was put above prudence, quackery above husbandry, 'scientific socialism' above the lessons of the years and the nature of man. In the prosecution of the class war the farmers were murdered or transported. It was like hijacking a ship and killing the crew. Economies of scale and improvements in machinery and methods were sensible, but those who transformed Soviet agriculture never realised that a bayonet makes a poor plough. Rather than submit to collectivisation many farmers destroyed their animals, killing them in such numbers that it took years for the herds to recover their former size. It was an epic of destruction that recalled the action of Muscovites when Napoleon reached their city in 1812. Rather than let the French take the city they burnt three-quarters of it, and Napoleon remarked with wonder on that particular Russian stubbornness.

There are some showcase collective and state farms. They are clean and efficient and go a long way to fulfilling the idea expressed in statues and posters of handsome workers bringing in the sheaves. But behind that veneer is a mass of farms lost in the past, in a swamp of sloth. More than a hundred and thirty years after the abolition of serfdom, many land workers remain little better than serfs. Farm bosses are much like the landlords of Tsarist times, but not so responsible and practical.

Where a Soviet farm worker feeds one person, his American counterpart feeds twelve. To produce a particular quantity of beef, a collective farm worker has to work fourteen times longer than an American. The emphasis is on rigid control from the centre, without regard for local conditions. Crises arise particularly at harvest time, because the system does not build enough tractors, combine harvesters or lorries and does not make enough batteries and spares for them. It does not train enough engineers to repair vehicles. In some places there is a lack of drivers. There is not enough fuel because the bungled management of the oil industry has created a petrol shortage. The inefficient operation of road and rail transport makes petrol delivery haphazard.

Ripe corn stretches to the horizon and trees are heavy with fruit. But a third of the crops rot in the ground, in storehouses, in lorries and in railway wagons shunted into sidings and forgotten. Packaging is non-existent and crops are battered in harvesting. Potatoes are left wet to rot. There are not enough grain stores, not enough vehicles to transport crops to storehouses and markets. So a grain-rich country has to buy grain abroad.

As the harvest neared, local authorities would order town-dwellers to the fields, an echo of an earlier era when students and factory workers and others were sent to the land to work for a pittance. People were angered at being used as cheap labour to get bad farm bosses out of a mess; and many factory managers were reluctant to disrupt production by letting workers go to the land. The amateur labour was, in any case, of doubtful value. Farm-workers complained that they spent too much time showing recruits how the job was done – and putting right their mistakes. Calling in the army was at best only a partial solution: the soldiers looked good on television, wielding sickles for the motherland. But the problem of storage and distribution remained.

One harvest time I travelled to the wheatlands of the Ukraine. Officials had stated there was 'a desperate need' for hands to gather the corn, and soldiers were helping out. A local policeman said to me: 'There is a crisis all right, but people do not believe that if they work harder it will be solved. Too much goes to waste and they are saying openly what they once used to whisper, that their leaders have no brains. Rotting food helps the nationalists because people blame Moscow.'

As the system of supply broke down some parts of the country kept the food they produced, refusing to channel it through the centralised network. People began to fend for themselves. Farms and factories dealt with each other, bartering machine parts for meat, cars for building materials. Republics began trading directly with one another, circumventing Moscow. When the cities ran short of food it was partly because their traditional suppliers in the country were keeping back meat, milk and vegetables to make sure that their own people had enough.

The cities have always been better off than the country. That is why people in outlying areas have had to travel to the city to buy food and clothing. Muscovites called the trains that arrived in the city from the neighbouring districts 'sausage trains' because they were full of countrywomen determined to secure supplies of saus-age. Country people who came to Moscow by bus were known as 'paratroopers' for the way they debouched from their transport and, wielding shopping bags, fanned out to assault the shops. The authorities in Moscow and other cities responded to local pressure and told shops to sell only to people who could produce a passport or identity card proving that they were city residents. But Soviet life has made people skilled in anarchy, finding loopholes and winking at regulations.

Empty shelves do not necessarily mean an empty shop. There is often trade at the back door. A shop may have nothing at the low price fixed by the state, but there may be goods under the counter at a higher price. Shops are supplemented by informal pavement stalls selling tomatoes, plums, tinned fruit, canned meat, sparrow-chested chickens. People dart towards them like shoals of fish, following the principle that you join the queue first and find out what is being sold afterwards. Everyone carries a bag of some kind, the never-know-your-luck bag, for everyone is a forager. The briefcases carried by thousands of men, including many in uniform, do not contain plans, reports and statistics; they are empty and their owners follow up any rumours of food.

Shortages have led to the growth of an informal intelligence network through which people track down supplies of food. Deliveries are notoriously haphazard and neither managers nor shoppers can tell when a store may receive a stock of cheese or pork, sausage or socks, dresses or overcoats. As soon as there is a delivery the word flashes around. One of the reasons it is so difficult to get through on the telephone to many offices and factories is that the network is operating, with women telling their friends and relations about deliveries and exchanging shopping information. For many people, survival would be impossible if they did not take time off work to queue. Occasionally the authorities refuse to recognise reality, and send police to check on queues and demand to know why people are not at work.

People have learnt to hoard. Cupboards are full of pasta, rice, flour and canned fish and soap. Balconies are meat stores. Bartering of goods is now commonplace: theatre tickets for meat, clothing for a car repair, a cheese for brandy. A man I knew kept vodka and pork joints in his car to buy machinery parts from factories. Although food often has to be found in the corners and shadowy places of the market, there remain certain lifelines. Factories and institutions receive supplies which they distribute to employees as a basic ration. Veterans and disabled people get special allowances, and children have school lunches.

I drove out to Zagorsk, forty-five miles from Moscow, one

December day to see how people were coping. The city authorities had imposed rationing, giving each person a monthly allowance of twelve eggs, half a pound of margarine, a pound of flour, a pound of cereal and half a pound of macaroni. In one of the state food shops a sign announced that carrots and potatoes would be limited. There was no fresh fish in the fish section, but an assistant said, 'We had some fish last week.' There was no meat for sale and the shelves were mostly bare except for yoghurt, fruit juice and dried fish. There was plenty of bread. There was also a great quantity of tea, but no one was buying it. When I asked why, a woman said 'It's Turkish, and there's a rumour going around that it was affected by a radiation cloud after the Chernobyl disaster.'

There was a butcher's shop, a private business which bought locally-raised meat from smallholders. Its prices were far higher than in the state shops but at least it had some supplies. On the day I was there it opened at 9 a.m. and within an hour had sold all its beef, pork and lamb. All that was left on the fresh meat counter was coypu – not to everyone's taste, but said to be delicious smoked or fried. A sign promised that it was good for children and for people with stomach trouble. The butcher said he bought about seven coypu a day.

The shoppers I met were resigned rather than angry. They expected their diet to be monotonous and, at times, sparse. 'It's terrible,' they said, 'but we are Russians and we get used to it.' A woman said:

I have stored enough food to last my family a month. Most people have built up a stock, it's common sense. But buying food becomes an obsession and you find yourself prowling around like a hunter. You keep in touch through the grapevine and get up early when you are tipped off about a sausage delivery. At the moment things are not too desperate. My husband eats at work and the children have school lunch. I found a piece of cheese in a shop in Moscow recently – that was a stroke of luck. It's my birthday today and I've saved up some Hungarian salami and chicken.

There is one area of Soviet agriculture which is successful, where crops and animals are raised with skill and care, where there is no difficulty with the harvest. The private plots of land on the margins of the collective and state farms, the kitchen gardens, cover only three per cent of the cultivable land but they provide a third of all the country's potatoes, half the vegetables, a fifth of its fruit, and significant quantities of meat. Chickens and pigs kept in backyards provide an important supplement to the diet and are the basis of a free-market economy. People sell their produce in the markets in all towns and cities, or to middlemen who run the stalls. The produce is of much higher quality than in the state shops. In the markets, cackling old women preside over potatoes and carrots, polishing their tomatoes and apples, garlic and greens. Men and women who make a living out of the favourite Russian hobby of mushroom-hunting stand with their forest hauls of chanterelles and other fungi. In the butchers' hall great joints are cut, rows of calves' heads stare out and women push suckling pigs forward for your attention. Many people cannot afford to shop in the markets, but the stalls are nevertheless thronged.

Alexei, one of the traders I met in the market near my home, showed me his morning's takings, a few rouble notes, crumpled and worn, smelling of the thousands of thumbs that had rubbed them. His grin revealed a few teeth standing up like bollards. 'I'm such a little fish,' he said, 'that I don't think the racketeers would give me a second glance.' Alexei worked in the flower section of the market. He was a distinctive figure in a worn leather jacket, his white hair covered with a flat cap made of brown fur, his snowy mandarin beard a good nine inches long. He lived about twelve miles from Moscow in one of those timeless, straggly villages of wooden tin-roofed houses and wooden fences. He grew tulips and gladioli bulbs and the seeds of other flowers. 'This proves I am an intelligent man,' he said. 'I can put all my produce into a suitcase and carry it to market. I couldn't do that if I grew potatoes, could I?'

On market days he rose at five in the morning, packed some bread and butter and a flask of tea and took the train to Moscow. Just after six he secured his favourite place on a white-tiled counter and paid £1.70 for his pitch. He set out his bulbs and seeds in small baskets with cards showing their names: 'Polar Bear', 'First Love', 'Baltic Amber' and 'Best Girl'. He chatted with the flower sellers around him and then he was ready to play his modest part in the budding free-enterprise economy which was seen by many of its hardline opponents as an ideological aberration. Alexei thought them wrong. He was a retired engineer and his pension did not stretch far enough. He had always been a gardener, and he turned his patch of land into a flower and fruit smallholding, sharing his strawberries, plums and blackcurrants among his family and getting his seven grandchildren and his great-grandson to help with the harvesting. Alexei said he liked Gorbachev. 'The good thing about him is that he encourages people to live like human beings, something we've all but forgotten how to do in this country. These days you don't have investigators sniffing about as you used to, and it is possible to believe in something again. In the old days, in Brezhnev's time, I did not dare to repair or paint my own house. If you made your house look pretty people resented it, they were jealous. They called you a profiteer.' Communism encouraged that mean streak summed up in the pithy Russian commentary: 'I wept because my cow had died, but I laughed because my neighbour's cow died, too.' Alexei said he would spend some of his profits on improving his seeds and growing roses for the cut-flower market. He would also paint his house.

★   ★   ★

Across the broad avenue from the market and up a narrow street stands an old banya. It leaks lazy plumes of steam, like a great saucepan on a hob. A friend and I went one day and for a rouble apiece bought bundles of birch leaves from a stall run by a toothless old woman. We roused the fat attendant slumbering in the office and bought tickets for a rouble.

The banya belongs to an older Moscow and older times and its grandeur is now dog-eared, its classical columns chipped and faded, its cupids yellowing and carpets thinning, its fine mosaics worn away. We ascended a curving staircase and entered a spacious changing-room with the wooden ceiling and heavy dark beams of a baronial hall. Rows of substantial benches were occupied by men senatorial in toga-like sheets. Some were sprawled, gossiping quiet-

ly or nibbling snacks of dried salt fish, some had just emerged from
the banya itself and sat looking beached, pink and panting.

There was a time when every village had its steam-bath and
travellers wrote of the Russians' delight in cooking themselves, and
steaming, and beating themselves with twigs before jumping into the
snow or an icy river. Russians thought of Europeans as bathless and
dirty.

We took up our birch switches and passed into the steamy gloom.
Scores of men moved slowly, soaping and scrubbing themselves with
close attention, flicking their legs and backs gently with their birch
leaves, like horses swishing their tails at flies. Sometimes coffee
grounds are used as an abrasive for back-scrubbing. We filled large
yellow plastic bowls with hot water from one of the gurgling taps on
the wall and found space on marble benches to place the bowls. We
soaped and scrubbed and rinsed and entered the hot room, a huge
Stygian wooden oven. We hopped like fire-walkers. In the centre of
the chamber rose a wide wooden staircase and the higher we
climbed the hotter the air became. Men chose their own levels on
the stairs and stood with heads bowed, as if contrite, running with
sweat, submitting silently to their ordeal. On the top level a few
heroes stood gasping, flipping their birch leaves over their shoulders
to make themselves sweat even more, tightening their lips as they
roasted and dripped. Old hands wore sopping brown felt hats they
had dunked in cold water before they entered the furnace. Properly
annealed, duty done and courage proved, we hopped our way
outside and hurried to plunge into the tepid water of the Roman
bath.

On the edge, among the yellowing columns, bathers talked
quietly. The banya is a steamy parliament in which there is no rank,
for nakedness and anonymity are equalisers. Only as men dressed
and resumed their outside shape and form did their conversation fall
away. They buttoned their mouths as they buttoned their shirts. In
the dressing-room we sat in rough white sheets and drank the beer
we had brought. Fathers checked that their small boys had washed
behind their ears.

Two pedicurists bent over their clients' feet, snipping nails and
filing hard skin and hooking out corns like a fishmonger opening
oysters. An old man with the build and lumbering gait of a

hippopotamus urged us to get our feet done. 'It costs only two roubles,' he said, 'and it makes your feet like new.' He lowered his voice and added confidentially: 'But take a tip from me – go to the older fellow on the right. He does a much better job, does it the old way. The young bloke does it the Soviet way and doesn't concentrate.'

He stood there, scratching his backside and grumbling about the way the country was governed. He jerked his thumb in the general direction of the Kremlin. 'Those people', he said, with a look of venom on his round Khrushchevian face, 'have been buggering us around from dawn to dusk for seventy years.'

★   ★   ★

In November we drifted in a grey limbo of sullen skies and sleety rain – 'No dawn, no dusk, no proper time of day'. On the lake in Gorky Park yellow pedalos crunched through the thin wafer of grey ice and the cold wind made cherries of children's noses. At the outdoor swimming pool bathers emerged from the tepid water to steam in the chill air, but one sensed that they were waiting for the full force of winter so that they could be really tested. November is a time of waiting, of impatient desire to lock horns with the foe. Skaters and cross-country skiers examine the weather forecasts and count the days. When the first snow falls and settles there is a feeling almost of relief. 'At last,' people say, 'now we can get on with it.'

When winter hardened its grip we put snow tyres on the car, unpacked our hats and boots and down-filled coats and taped the windows of the flat against draughts, leaving just the small corner window, the *fortochka*, to be opened for ventilation. The blanket of snow softened the noise of traffic. Snowploughs went to work and snow was gathered up into a truck by the 'capitalist', a contraption with two crab-like arms and a grabbing, croupier motion. Workmen shovelled snow into high ramparts beside the road. Tough men and women used outsize jemmies to keep the tramline points free of ice.

I continued my walks in the Hermitage gardens. Grandparents would still be out with the prams, the babies lying wrapped up like bandaged thumbs. All the parks were lovely in the snow. At dusk one day, in Sokolniki Park, the graceful birches had a silvery gleam and I found myself drawn along the snowy path by distant music and a faint glow of light seen through spindly branches. As I emerged from the trees I felt I had found a hidden corner, a secret Moscow, as if I had stumbled upon the teddy bears' picnic. There was an open-air arena and its perimeter was banked high with snow and lit by a corona of red, blue and yellow lights. The arena was full of people, a dark moving mass, bulky and ursine in fur and leather coats, their thick scarves, gloves and heavy boots and fur hats sprinkled with snowflakes. They were all middle-aged or elderly people, and here in this freezing place they whirled beneath the indigo sky to the sensuous Latin rhythms of the tango. They held their heads proudly, placed their steps expertly and gravely, and when the dance ended, the music fading tinnily on the loudspeakers, the greying gentlemen bowed to their ladies with the stiff politeness of young officers at a ball. The frosty air was suffused with romance. The band struck up again and the dancers swept away into waltz and foxtrot, quickstep and tango. The music was in the style of Victor Silvester alternating with Glenn Miller. There were rather more women than men and a few of them danced together, gliding across the sanded ice 'as stately as a galleon' in their fur coats. But no one was really a wallflower and women standing on the edge of the arena did not have to wait long before some gallant old blade appeared, offering a strong arm and a polite and smiling 'Excuse me, may I . . .?' and they would be drawn away into the throng. A woman told me she came every weekend to dance. Dancing in the dark was very romantic, she said, and it kept her warm. Besides, it cost only fifty kopecks.

However bitter the weather, Moscow's artists and craftsmen set up their tables and stalls in the weekend art market near Ismailova Park and people turn out in force to browse and buy. There is the distinctive sound of boots crunching on the crisp piecrust snow. Napoleon's retreat from Moscow must have sounded like this. The artists and doll makers are red-faced and blue-nosed, suffering for art and commerce, propping up their pictures with twigs stuck in the snow, putting them up again when the wind blows them over. They bang their feet and huddle together, lighting cigarettes. Someone opens a tin box and begins to sell hot pastries, the irresistible bakery smell making nostrils quiver in 'Ah, Bisto' fashion. Kebabs splutter on a barbecue and even on the most bitter day there is a line at an ice-cream stall and people queuing to buy mouldy-looking frost-damaged tangerines.

The market is popular because it is a place to buy something in a society where there is little to spend roubles on. It is also popular with foreigners and is one of the doorways through which foreign currency enters the economy. Spread out on cloths and newspapers on the snow are brass candlesticks, old cameras, coins, clocks, icons, religious books, crucifixes, lithographs of churches. People have been searching their attics and cupboards to bring out jewel-lery, postcards of Old Moscow and portraits of the last Tsar and his family. There is intense interest in such mementoes. A man will stand all day hoping to sell a single samovar. Puppet-makers jiggle their marionettes, carvers display painted eggs, toy soldiers and chess sets. Furniture-makers set out small tables and bookcases. Egg-shaped old women stand by stalls selling home-made lace and thick socks and mittens, looking as if they have modelled for the *matryoshkas*, the nesting sets of wooden dolls which are the definitive Russian souvenir.

Of late, satirical matryoshkas have become a minor art form, popular with foreigners who are usually the only people who can afford them. There are Gorbachev dolls, Yeltsin dolls, Stalin dolls and dolls of KGB men with horrible gargoyle faces and daggers dripping blood. Inside a Gorbachev doll there is a bushy-browed Brezhnev with an iconostasis of medals on his chest and another array on his back. Inside Brezhnev is Khrushchev, holding a corn-cob as a mark of his farm-boy origins, and behind his back he clutches a shoe, the one he banged theatrically on the table at the United Nations in 1962. Inside Khrushchev is Stalin, pipe in one hand and an axe in the other; and concealed in Stalin's wooden womb is a thimble-sized Lenin holding a copy of his newspaper, *The Spark*; and behind his back is one of the decrees with which he changed Russia.

In winter, as well as the crunch of boots, there is the hiss of skis in the parks and the rasp of skates on paths flooded to make skating trails. Beside the river, in the silvery wood, I skied inexpertly among the spinneys and tumbled down the slopes, watched by contemptuous, expert children. When I walked among the naked trees the black crows hopped in the branches behind me, croaking and signalling and flitting, keeping watch, like spies in black cloaks, ghosts of the KGB. Walking across the frozen river I watched anglers drill holes through the ice with augers and then settle for a long wait, their faces set like those of sentries. I glanced over the shoulders of artists who stuck their easels into the snow and painted with crabbed and frozen fingers the scenes they would sell in the pavement art markets.

In the last days of December men and women hunt in the markets for the little fir tree, the *yolka*, that is decorated for Christmas by believers and for the New Year festival by everyone. Children await a visit from Grandfather Frost, a hearty, Falstaffian fellow with a white beard, a red tunic and a sack of toys, usually an actor rented by parents for a few roubles and often a graduate of a Grandfather Frost school where courses set a standard of behaviour. This version of Santa Claus is attended by a Snow Maiden who has the secretarial role of ensuring that Grandfather Frost keeps his appointments and does not drink too much. In December people assiduously accumulate food, wine, vodka and gifts for the New Year dinner and for the uninhibited party that lasts until dawn and lights a beacon on the way to distant and ached-for spring.

It is the puddly season. The ramparts of packed snow beside the roads melt away. Icicles shatter on the pavements. Workmen are dispatched with shovels to the roofs and push the softening snow to the streets. Days and nights conspire in treachery, thawing and freezing, so that the streets are more slippery than in winter. Roads are foul with slush and mud and in the countryside merge with the fields in one swampy mess.

Then one day people arrive from the country with catkins, like messengers bearing notes saying that spring is really in sight. Suddenly, as if there has been a decree from the Kremlin, people leave off their fur hats. We can see the girls' faces again. There is less work for the cloakroom women to do. Spring is a dam-burst, the rush of a swollen river. There is a sudden abundance of flowers in the markets, a profusion of lilac and lilies of the valley, and the air is heavy with an intoxicating scent. The parks become green almost overnight, lush and overgrown.

On Friday evenings the Moscow ring road is full of cars heading for the countryside, for the family dacha, the house, cottage, shack or hut which for many people is their escape and relief, something that makes life worth living. Going to the dacha is an animal migration, a return to roots, for most Russians are only a generation or two away from a rural existence. The dacha is often a green-painted wooden house in a village or hamlet. It has window frames and shutters carved with designs of flowers and leans half-capsized in an unkempt garden with a Jack-and-Jill well near the crooked wooden fence. Chickens roam in the streets and ducks march platoons of young to the pond. The dacha is a base for mushroom-gathering, a patch for growing flowers, vegetables and fruit. But it is not a place for mowing the lawn, for grass is loved and therefore uncut; I never saw a lawnmower in Russia. A dacha is never finished and is always being repaired, patched, painted and rebuilt. There is nothing half so much worth doing as simply messing about in dachas. The cars leaving for the country carry tools, fabrics, pieces of timber, glass and metal for making improvements. They also carry a can or two of petrol so that the family can get back home.

When the sun shines people in Moscow head for the river beaches. On hot days the river is brown and cool and flows in lazy swirls. Some of the swimmers are the sort of knotty old boys and stalwart old girls who plunge in every day of the year. On patches of worn grass men and women play volleyball with a holiday-camp gusto; large ruminant grandmothers, unabashed and formidable in heroic brassières and majestic bloomers, rule the family picnic rugs, cutting black bread and sausage and setting out jars of salted cucumbers. Haughty girls stroll by in bikinis, absorbing all the sunlight they can get and the appreciative glances which are their due. Summer is brief and people offer themselves to the sun, reddening gladly, stretching their necks upwards like sunflowers to get closer to the heat. There is not much noise, no radios playing.

Fathers rig hammocks in the silver birch trees and allow the torpid afternoons to slip through their fingers while they eat cold potatoes from a bowl, and swig from jars of thin fruit juice. The industrious practise their origami, making sun-hats out of *Pravda*.

In Gorky Park, too, there is a certain seemliness, enjoyment taken in a grave and undemonstrative way. The summer air lies hot and heavy and dusty. On the boating lake no one bends to the oars very much and the occupants of the slowly drifting boats are reflected and reflective. Gorky Park, the Soviet Union's first 'park of culture and rest', is one of Moscow's favourites. At weekends it costs thirty kopecks to get in and the tickets are taken by members of the corps of elderly ladies who, with sharp concierge glances, keep doors all over Moscow. Sometimes there is a brass band playing under the triumphal archway at the entrance, but the music is soon swallowed in the trees and gives way to the tweeting of the bird whistles that small boys buy as soon as they get in. Fortunately they tire of being thrushes after a minute or two. There are other pools of noise – the squawk of the puppet show, a clamour round the circus big top, a burst of song from a stage – but it is easy to find a quiet dappled glade or avenue where the ice-cream eaters sit and stroll, absorbed in pleasure, licking thoughtfully and abstractedly. Middle-aged and elderly men wear medals and ribbons on their best suits, grandmothers are in bright prints, little girls have large bows in their hair. Pretty young women in smart dresses with half-stockings reaching to the knee swing along on heels so high your own feet ache in sympathy. Many of them look a picture as they promenade through the park, attracting the admiring stares of sauntering soldiers.

Women take great pains to keep up appearances. Clothing in state shops is usually dowdy and ill-made. Stylish clothes are hard to find, and each woman has to be her own patient sleuth in hunting down materials, threads and buttons. They and their dressmakers spend hours studying and copying designs seen in the rare Western magazines, passed around until they grow grubby. When a Russian city ran short of black dress material, women were told they would have to prove that a relative had died and that they were in mourning before they would be allowed to buy black.

Part of Gorky Park is a fairground, its famous ferris wheels its badge. On the Wall of Death daring young men on their motorbikes whizz around like roulette balls. They fling up their arms and slip on blindfolds before rounding off their act with a flourish and salute. There is a polite smacking of applause and the spectators, mildly thrilled, walk out into the sunshine. People queue to enter a large drum and when it spins round they are pinned to the wall by centrifugal force. In the West people would squeal, but the spreadeagled Russians endure in expressionless silence like initiates in a tribal rite, and when the centrifuge slows and stops they leave quietly without chatter. Dodgem cars are driven sedately, as if one of Moscow's traffic policemen were ready to jump out with his white wand and catalogue of petty laws. Artists set themselves up in the shade and people line up to have their portraits made in chalk, charcoal or pencil. Children pose in fidgetless obedience.

The zoo, too, is a favourite outing, an oasis in the heart of the city, watched over by tall trees and encroached on by a jungle of unruly greenery. It is a haunt of courting couples, who drift arm-in-arm eating ice-cream or sit in grubby cafés nibbling brown bread and floppy sausage, sipping glasses of weak beer made from fermented rye bread.

I went to the zoo one day during the season of *pookh*, the time in June when the air in Moscow is full of white fluffy specks of feathery poplar seeds, like those of the dandelion. They form wispy snowlike drifts in doorways and detonate sneezes among allergic watery-eyed pookh martyrs. The zoo seemed all of a piece with Moscow and with modern Russian life. There was a paucity of animals, but perhaps it was no bad thing: the zoo was founded in 1864 and the cages are old-fashioned and cramped, with black iron bars. Many of them were empty, rusted and cracked, falling apart and overgrown with weeds. The concrete elephant compound had no inhabitant. A knot of people stared contemplatively into the space, as if imagining an elephant. At other empty compounds, too, they had to rely on their memories. An aviary roof had collapsed and many of the enclosures, occupied by goats, deer and birds, were jungles of nettles, long grass and weeds. A large number of the buildings were built of wood and looked like cottages in the country. They were down-at-heel and contributed to the zoo's air of desuetude; and so did some of the keepers and assistants who shuffled in a desultory round-shouldered way with buckets and brooms and metal containers of foul meat.

In his small cage a large shaggy brown bear paced restlessly up and down, banging his body on one wall and then the other, the picture of frustration in confinement, a sad condition for the symbol of the Slavs' mightiest pagan god. In the adjoining cage, too mean a cell for his handsome and supple body, a tiger roamed to and fro, tormented by teenage boys. They had wriggled through the outer railings and were drumming on the mesh of the cage with their fingers, a tantalising inch from the tiger's nose. In the reptile house a man showed off to his family by flicking a yo-yo covered in lime-green nylon fur in front of an alligator. The alligator's snout was pressed to the glass of his tank and he opened one amber eye and gave the yo-yonik a long, level glance. Perhaps when they slumber the creatures of Moscow zoo dream of biting off a few heads. The reptile house was newly-built, but like so many new Soviet structures it had a slightly discoloured and dog-eared look, as if deliberately pre-aged. Before its opening the amphibian colony was in distress: the old quarters were so derelict that the cold of winter threatened to kill all the creatures. Compassionate zoo-keepers brought in hot-water bottles for them and the chief croco-dile was roped and carried to a temporary and warmer ark. But the crocodiles as a group rebelled at the cold and disturbance and went off their food. A hunger strike, one of the Soviet newspapers called it.

If there were few animals in the zoo, there were many in the pet market near Taganka Square. There were hundreds of dogs for sale. The most fashionable, such as Afghan hounds and bull terriers, were selling for more than a hundred pounds. For a small-time breeder, happiness could be a pregnant dachshund. A writer in *Pravda* pursed his lips over such naked capitalism and wrote of the need for the state to control dog prices. The pet market had become a place of permitted small-scale capitalism and breeding dogs and cats for money was just as much a business as growing fruit and veget-ables or raising a pig for private sale. It was one place where people could spend money and it had its niche in the free market that was filling the gaps in the state-run economy. The money made from the sale of a poodle pup is spent on better food or a better coat.

Once through the dog line I entered the avenue of cats. Patient women stood shoulder to shoulder, shifting from foot to weary foot, holding their animals. At their feet were bags and boxes full of kittens, sleeping or cuffing each other and looking like models for sentimental calendars. I could have bought a good mouser for a few roubles.

The market was crowded, thousands of people shoving gently and purposefully. It was a scruffy place on rough and puddly ground and full of ramshackle stalls. Dusty trams, the colour of tangerines, rattled across one end. As well as the dog and cat sellers there were hundreds of men and women with tanks of exotic fish and a long line of people who seemed to stand all day holding jars of iridescent minnows. There were bird-mongers, too, with canaries and budgerigars in tiny home-made wooden cages. There were ducks for sale, and doves, terrapins, snakes, tortoises, cocks, hens, hamsters and teeming mounds of maggots, the smoky piddly air filled with barking, yapping, mewing, clucking, squeaking and trilling.

The authorities have been trying to close down the pet market for years on health grounds, if not for ideological reasons, but the people have made it clear they like it the way it is. It is a popular institution and belongs to the people in a particular way, a place of their own, animated and diverting.

Like the pet market, the Moscow racecourse is part of the private life of the Russian public, a hidden world, a haven from the treadmill and the queue, from absurdity and censoriousness. Racing was frowned on by the communists, which no doubt made it more attractive, and it has never been covered in the papers or shown on television.

The opening of the flat-racing season in May rings up the curtain on summer for racing fans. When I went, paying forty kopecks at the guichet to get in and another twenty-five for a programme, it was a sunny and breezy afternoon and the crowd and the atmosphere put me in mind of Brighton in the holidays. The hippodrome is an immense stadium, constructed in 1883, and the main building, housing the stands, is a huge caramel-coloured structure of dowdy grandeur. It rises in a pseudo-classical style and its tower is surmounted by equine statues, just like the prancing horses which adorn Russian painted trays. The entrance is a marbled hall and staircases lead to vast rooms with columns and painted ceilings, so that every punter can feel he is touched by Tsarist extravagance. The more comfortable and expensive sections of the grandstand have stained-glass windows.

The crowd was relaxed and good-natured. Most of the men wore open-necked shirts, the young men jeans and leather jackets. Some people sported hats fashioned from newspapers. I saw only one policeman and he was lounging with a cigarette, tormenting nobody and not even toying with his stick. Almost everyone seemed to be smoking, as people used to in the West in the carefree days before cancer warnings, and old men lit up and coughed vigorously to expel the fresh air from their lungs. Several men were cadging from their friends because of a cigarette shortage caused partly by the failure of a factory to produce enough filter tips. But one of the tobacco factories was circumventing this difficulty by manufacturing cigarettes without filters and, with sardonic humour, giving them the brand name of 'Risk'.

A brass band in front of the grandstand played jauntily on battered trumpets and trombones, with one musician wrapped in a dented sousaphone. In front of us, horses were put through their pre-race paces by jockeys in gaudy, rippling silks. Seven of the thirteen events on the card were to be trotting races and the jockeys were perched on frail buggies, their legs wide apart and their faces close to the quick-strutting hooves of the horses. The large crowd was predominantly male but there were a number of strikingly glamorous women, smartly-dressed and walking on high heels with the gliding elegance of giraffes. Some of them had arty escorts, young men in Italian jackets with their hair tied in queues.

The afternoon started with a parade, as in a circus, led by skittish horses ridden by men and women in black riding habits and hats. There was a splash of Tsarist pageantry as riders trotted by in hussar's uniforms, bright red and bottle-green. The horses were lively and two of the dashing moustachioed hussars were tossed humiliatingly onto the sandy soil. A pair of troikas, chariots drawn by three horses abreast, rattled by and then the racehorses paraded, stepping impatiently. The crowd cheered and even the serious punters glanced up. They had been absorbed in their race pro-grammes and in their home-made form books, thick volumes filled with notes and codes. They consulted these inky compendiums with deep concentration and marked their programmes with squiggles, compiling elaborate compound bets. I did not understand the system but the simplest bet was to pick the horses that would come first and second. It was not enough to pick the winner, and there was no such thing as an each-way bet. A man explained how to make a simple bet and added, darkly, 'I'm not saying that the jockeys agree in advance who will win . . . but everyone knows that they like caviare.'

In the cavern beneath the grandstand there were long lines at the betting guichets. There were no individual bookmakers, for betting is controlled by the state, but there were knots of men hunched in conspiratorial groups. All the betting clerks were women, known as bukmakeri, and once they had punched the detail of bets into computers, the machines spat out betting slips. It is one of the few operations in the Soviet Union, outside the defence industry and the KGB, which is efficiently computerised.

The first race was about to start. The horses, bred in the Ukraine and the Caucasus, looked splendid to my untutored eye, but a note in the race programme said rather wistfully that 'our horses cannot rival the best American and European bloodstock and this limits our prospects of exporting them. Nevertheless we are frequently invited to foreign races.' The crowd erupted excitedly as the horses dashed past the post marked with the English word 'Finish' written in Cyrillic script. I was uncertain whether I had won anything and went to the payout desk. 'Not this time,' said the bukmaker, softening the pain with a smile.

Ira, our cheerful and resourceful cook-housekeeper, introduced us to many Russian dishes and coped with domestic emergencies. When the sink overflowed and flooded the kitchen floor, as it did from time to time, she called in the local handyman, and when he had finished I rewarded him with a tumblerful of neat gin which he drank in a single gulp. One day, when I enquired about small circular sticking-plasters on her arms, Ira said she had consulted a faith healer who had promised her that the plasters, affixed in certain places, would reduce her appetite and her weight.

Healers, folk doctors and herbalists are numerous and popular. Many people receive little help from the inefficient health service and a healer may be their only hope. I saw one at work when I stopped one day at a farm on the road from Riga to Vilnius. A dozen people sat on benches and boxes in the farmyard watching turkeys strut up and down while they waited to see Aunt Arina, the famous local healer. One of the women said she had travelled 120 miles that day because Aunt Arina was renowned and because her doctor had not been able to help her. Aunt Arina held her surgery in the stone-floored kitchen, her chair beside the window and beneath some nets of onions, her patients sitting opposite her across the stout table. She was a white-haired dumpling of ninety with bright and intelligent eyes. She had large strong hands and wore a blue cardigan and an orange apron over her flower-print dress. She told me that she made her own medicines from herbs she gathered in her garden or in the fields and hedges. 'Many of the cases I see are not too difficult to diagnose. People become ill because of their bad diet and it is obvious that a lot of sickness around here is caused by pollution and the pesticides sprayed onto crops. The medicines I make can help, but I cannot fight the pollution.' A woman working as her receptionist said that Aunt Arina had seen 17,000 patients in two years. 'They come because they have faith in her. Once, some officials came to stop her practising. They were rude. They said: "What can this old granny do for people?" But they couldn't stop the people seeing her. They couldn't close her down because they couldn't provide anything to put in her place.'

At the time I lived in Moscow, two men who promoted themselves as healers had extraordinary careers on television. They became the talk of the land and when their programmes were on the air it seemed that the city streets were deserted. One of them was Alan Chumak, who claimed to have harnessed a force with healing properties that he could transmit to water and paper. He instructed his television audience to place glasses of water in front of their sets, saying that the water would be charged with 'bio-energy' and, when consumed, would cure their ailments. A scientist reported that he had been able to measure this energy. When Chumak said he had transmitted his energy to a particular edition of a Moscow newspaper, the edition quickly sold out and people put pieces of the paper in water to make a curative drink or a balm for wounds. People journeyed for hundreds of miles from all parts of the country to see Chumak, and a crowd waited every morning outside his flat in Moscow.

He was rivalled by Anatoly Kashpirovsky, of saturnine appearance and burning gaze who, as a hypnotist and bringer of hope, had millions hanging on his words. In his television shows he promised the sick that their insomnia would disappear, their lameness vanish, their tumours recede, their sight return; and, sure enough, people appeared on the show to report to audiences of millions that they were cured. Many people felt a sudden surge of emotion while watching his programme, and burst spontaneously into tears.

The popularity of these healers was perhaps a symptom of a society under stress and filled with uncertainty. Both had supporters in high places, and both gave bizarre press conferences at the foreign ministry, part of the aim being to excite foreign interest in their work and to attract investment. When I went to Kashpirovsky's conference the press hall was overflowing, but three-quarters of those jostling for seats were the wives, daughters, mothers and aunts of government employees, trying to see their hero. To get a seat myself I had to ask a woman to put her little girl on her lap. Kashpirovsky wore a leather jacket and cast his intense gaze over the audience. 'I'm not a magician,' he protested (although his admirers clearly thought he was), 'but I can reverse what was thought to be irreversible. I tap the inner resources of the body.' He said that under his influence scars faded away. A little later I was surprised when a Russian I had thought rather hard-headed told me: 'It's true. It may be his eyes, the way he stares, but I had a scar on my arm and after I'd watched his show it went away.'

For a while Chumak and Kashpirovsky were a sensation. Some scientists dismissed them as mountebanks, as latter-day Rasputins (Grigori Rasputin was the Siberian mystic who acquired a sinister influence with the last Empress of Russia after he treated her haemophiliac son). But the sceptics could say what they liked. The gurus were dealing in hope, with the emotions of people who found their doctors inconsiderate and unable to provide drugs and other treatments. In any case, communism had not destroyed the fascination with folk beliefs, mysticism and cures, any more than religion completely swept away pagan ideas.

The phenomenal rise of the television healer was part of an abiding enthusiasm for the paranormal. Russians are endlessly entertained and intrigued by reports of unidentified flying objects and there is as great an interest in UFOs as there is in the United States. Encounters with extraterrestrial beings are frequently reported and seriously discussed in the press. Creatures wearing silver space suits and staring about them with three eyes seem to be regular visitors to parts of central and southern Russia.

The yeti is another favourite mystery. Everyone knows from reports of encounters that the yeti is hairy and amazingly strong. Every August intrepid teams of explorers head off to remote mountains in search of the yeti, what Russian scientists call 'the relic humanoid'. Every September the teams return, having found nothing of any importance. There are all manner of research groups investigating sightings in the Pamirs, the Urals and the fastnesses of Central Asia, and every now and then there are discoveries of giant footprints. The last time I read about a yeti expedition the leader described his quarry as tall, hairy, jug-eared and with impressive biceps, a creature able to manipulate the human mind from a distance. Healers, flying saucers and yetis provide for many a romance and mystery without which life seems incomplete.

In my office the anchor was Nellie, my vivacious secretary, whose name was the diminutive of Ninel, Lenin backwards, one of the few Soviet, as opposed to Russian, names, bestowed at one time on many children. One snowy morning, as she was on her way to work, Nellie was in a car crash and she was pulled from the wreck and taken to hospital. When I went to see her she was in a ward with five other women who had been seriously injured in road accidents. The ward was none too clean and two of the women were groaning piteously. Nothing reflects the bad conditions and shortages in Soviet hospitals as much as the way a nurse took the bloodstained bandage from the head of one patient and rewound it on the head of another.

I had been to Soviet hospitals before and knew what to expect. I had met doctors, dedicated men and women, who told me about the state of health care, so I was not surprised that used bandages were being recycled. The best doctors and nurses, and clinics with Western equipment and medicines, were reserved for the nomen-klatura, the Communist Party élite. Major surgery was generally available only to those in the hierarchy. Health care for the bulk of the people had a low priority. After decades of being run on the cheap the health service has serious shortages of even simple primary equipment and, in many places, extremely poor standards of care and hygiene. Hospitals and other institutions are a mirror of society at large, reflecting the contempt the authorities have for the people. But there are exceptions. At a home for the disabled in Moscow I was moved by the compassion of staff, particularly those who looked after Marya and Darya, known by their diminutives as Masha and Dasha, who are Siamese twins joined at the waist, two people sharing one pair of legs. When they were born forty-two years ago doctors took them away to conduct research on them and told their mother they had died. Like most of the disabled in Russia the twins were hidden away in a home for the mentally handicap-ped. Then they lived in a dental hospital before moving to the home where I met them. They were nearly forty before they met their mother and found that they had two brothers.

They have emerged from all this extraordinarily cheerful and spirited, with impish smiles and a ready wit. They showed me their private flat and their electric wheelchair, a gift from Germany.

We've survived [said Masha] because we laugh a lot and we've accepted the fact that as we are inseparable we shouldn't fight too much. When we were young it took us years to learn to sit up and to walk because our nervous systems are so compli-cated. With us, co-ordination is everything – how do you think we keep the flat swept and polished?

It would be boring if we had the same temperament. I'm

more cheerful and Dasha is more serious. We disagree quite
often in discussion but we don't come to blows as we did when
we were little. We don't always like the same things on
television and if I'm watching sport Dasha will read a book or
fall asleep. But we both like serious novels and the good
newspapers like *Argumenty i Fakty*.

Life has been better for us since Gorbachev took over
because the feeling went around that things should change. We
ourselves said that we shouldn't be hidden away, that the
disabled deserved something better. We kicked up a fuss and
people began to help us. That's how we got to this place, which
is a great improvement. The director and some of the staff have
become our friends. It's been a struggle, but it always has been.
We've had to be brave from the first day of our lives.

But compassion cannot make up for a lack of medicine and
equipment. When I went to Armenia after the earthquake which
killed 25,000 people, I met a doctor in one of the wrecked cities who
told me that he and others rushed to the disaster where, in the
nightmare of wreckage and injured, they found themselves helpless:
they had no emergency equipment, no drugs, no pain-killers, no
saline drips, no plasma, no antiseptics, no bandages, no splints, no
syringes. 'I had a handkerchief and a penknife,' he said.

The élite had not only better medical attention but also a better
diet, buying in special shops from which the majority were excluded.
The declining standards of health care and their dietary deficiencies
put the ordinary people of the country at third-world levels. The
Soviet Union has the lowest life-expectancy of any developed
country. Men can expect to live to sixty-four. In Khrushchev's time
the expectation of life was sixty-seven. A miner's life expectancy is
forty-eight and only five per cent of miners live to draw their
pensions. Infant mortality, a significant measure of health in any
society, is rising; and although the figures are affected by the high
mortality rates in Soviet Central Asia, the number of babies who die
in the first year of life in the Soviet Union is very much higher than
in the West, a reflection of the health of mothers and the standards
of nutrition as well as of low standards of hospital hygiene and bad
housing.

The shortage of medicines is everywhere acute because the pharmaceutical industry is as badly run as any other industry under the central command system. A box of Western pain-killers or a proprietary influenza remedy is a welcome gift for many Russians. People make a point of keeping on good terms with pharmacists. Drugs sell for high prices on the black market and if someone is ill and in need of certain medicines his relatives spend days hunting for them. Medicines smuggled out of the nomenklatura hospitals sell for large sums. If they can afford it, people entering hospital take enough money to bribe the nursing and medical staff to give them better care. If they are fortunate their relatives bring them decent food. The shortage of anaesthetics means that many minor operations are done without them. Most doctors are poorly paid and receive wages a third below the national average. They often take other jobs to make ends meet and have little choice but to take the bribes for treatment and operations. Much of their equipment is outdated and they lack such basic tools as sharp scalpels and disposable syringes. The country manufactures only one billion disposable syringes a year: it needs at least six billion. It fails to make enough cotton wool and dressings. A sixth of Soviet hospitals lack running water and nearly half are without running hot water. Almost a quarter have no sewerage system and about half lack baths and showers. Half have no diagnostic X-ray equipment. In rural hospitals conditions are almost always worse than in the cities.

The pattern of disease reflects the poor living conditions. Typhoid, paratyphoid, diphtheria, meningitis and tuberculosis afflict many thousands of people. Fresh vegetables and fruit are unavailable to many Russians except during the harvest weeks, and millions of people suffer vitamin deficiency. The Soviet suicide rate is one of the highest in the world, and is increasing.

The Soviet Union boasts of its large number of health workers: forty-four doctors per 10,000 people, for example, compared with twenty in Britain; and while some Soviet doctors are excellent, many are the low-grade products of inadequate training. When a journalist colleague of mine became seriously ill with a congenital heart defect, two doctors who arrived to see him did not even possess an instrument for measuring blood pressure. He was eventually taken to a squalid hospital where bloodstained bandages lay on the floor and the staff were unsympathetic and even hostile. When his wife and friends found him cold and shivering they brought warmer clothes, but these were refused and they were told that his being cold would help him. When a friend managed to see him, in spite of the resistance of the staff, he found him thirsty and in pain. He had asked for tea but none had been brought. The friend asked the staff to bring some but was told sharply, 'He's already had juice.' A cup of tea was finally carried in with ill grace. It was cold. My colleague died two hours later. His wife asked to see him but the staff said this was not possible. She persisted and was directed by an impatient nurse to a stretcher lying in the corridor. On it was her husband's body. The staff were indifferent throughout. 'And that, of course,' Russians said, 'is how they treat everybody.'

The man's friends went to a state coffin depot where the woman in charge abused them for disturbing her at 4.30 in the afternoon. To get a coffin they paid a bribe of two hundred roubles, equivalent to her pay for a month. It is almost impossible to arrange a funeral without bribery. A coffin must be secured (party officials and their families have priority) and the grave-diggers given vodka or cash to make a proper grave.

The grave-diggers had, mercifully, done their job well when I attended the funeral of an ordinary man one chilly afternoon. The coffin lay in the back of a battered yellow bus provided by the state undertakers, the Bureau of Ritual Servicing. Family and friends were crowded into the uncomfortable seats and the driver had the unmistakable look of a bored delivery man as he drew on his cigarette. The bus trundled far beyond the Moscow city limits and turned onto an unmarked road over brown heathland. There used to be a sign pointing to the cemetery but it was taken down years ago because, the story goes, the cemetery lies off the road to the VIP airport and Brezhnev did not like to see the sign every time he went to catch a plane. The cemetery, bordered by a concrete wall and dotted with rough green privies, is the largest in Moscow and has more than half a million graves.

The funeral bus halted and the coffin, covered in a bright red cloth, was removed through a small rear door and placed on a trolley. The mourners formed a procession led by one of the relatives holding a placard which bore the name of the dead man and a short printed tribute. The man's mother sang a chant of grief. As the procession moved off five portly middle-aged men in shapeless suits, with medals on their chests, put trumpets and cornets to their lips and blew a funeral march. The cortège followed a lane through the birch trees and reached the grave. The coffin was opened for a few minutes, for a eulogy and final farewells, and was then hammered shut and lowered into the grave. One of the mourners carried a curlicued metal cross to mark the place until a permanent gravestone could be erected, perhaps bearing a photograph or etched portrait.

Russians take respectful care of their dead, one reason why the indifference and scruffiness of the state funeral undertakings cause such resentment. Graves are for the most part well-tended and families often plant a sapling by the grave, so many cemeteries are pleasantly wooded. Funerary rituals are strongly maintained. As I walked through the cemetery I saw many women keeping vigil, sitting on stools set beside the graves. They come to talk to the dead and stay for hours, often leaving morsels of food on small tables. At the meal after a funeral, a place and chair are set aside for the deceased. A glass of vodka is poured and kept for forty days, evaporating slowly. Traditionally there is a visit to the grave nine days after a death, and a memorial meal on the fortieth day. At Easter thousands go in family groups to visit graves. If the sun shines they sit all day, talking and picnicking.

Part of the cemetery I visited, the Khovanskoye, is set aside for soldiers. Some of the graves were of men killed in action in Afghanistan. During the war relatives were not permitted to mention that fact on a headstone, and the words 'Patriot and Internationalist' served as a code. The authorities wanted to hide the fact that thousands of men were killed. The furtive and dishonest way they treated the dead rankles with families to this day.

The Khovanskoye is a cemetery for ordinary Muscovites. Heroes and leaders lie in the Kremlin wall. Vagankovskoye is a traditional resting place for writers, while the KGB took their secrets to the grave at Kuntsevo, as Kim Philby did. The best Moscow necropolis is beside the Novodevichy monastery. Gogol and Chekhov lie here, along with many other writers and poets, and some of the nobility of pre-revolutionary Russia. The graves of party stalwarts, generals, inventors and others are surmounted by examples of remarkable funerary art in the Soviet Heroic style. Statues and busts incorporate symbols of the deceased's achievements – an aircraft for a designer, a microphone for a broadcaster, a circus costume for a clown. In the hands of a famous obstetrician lies a new-born child. Khrushchev's grave is marked by a larger-than-life bronze of his turnip head. Stalin's second wife, Alliluyeva, who killed herself in 1932, is here, too. Beneath the marble carving of her sad face I saw a tribute of fresh flowers.

★   ★   ★

Our office driver, Tolya, was a very good driver indeed. As such, he was exceptional. Driving standards in the Soviet Union are poor and, by my observation, were growing worse as people became more aggressive. More than 61,000 people are killed on Soviet roads every year, compared with 50,000 in the United States where there are ten times more vehicles. About a sixth of the people injured in road accidents subsequently die in hospital because emergency services and accident treatment are bad.

The pleasures of Soviet motoring are few. To acquire or achieve anything connected with private transport is to struggle with bureaucracy, battle with sharks in the black market, fight corruption and scrounge for parts. Everything is in short supply: cars, spare parts, windscreen wipers, tyres, oil, petrol. A Russian I knew had been on the waiting list for a car for ten years, although I also knew people who had bought one after being on a list for only five or six years. The cheapest car is the small Zaparozhets, which is often issued to invalids. The people's car is the Zhiguli, exported for desperately-needed foreign currency under the name of Lada. Next up the scale are the Moskvitch and the Volga. Many Volgas are used as official cars and there is an enormous caste of chauffeurs, some of whom use the cars as taxis while the boss is at a meeting. Ambulance drivers, too, do some moonlighting in their ambulances. The largest cars, the Chaika and Zil, are not for sale and are reserved for the élite. The massive Zil is the state chariot. Between ten and twenty-five of them are built every year.

It is not possible to go to a showroom because car sales are made through government departments, factories and institutions, and each organisation has an allocation. Some are more equal than others, and in vital factories and institutions the waiting list is much shorter. It is not enough for a person to put himself on the list and then wait. In common with the process of waiting for other expensive goods, he may be required to attend at an office from time to time to reassert his claim. It is therefore a red-letter day when a citizen surfaces at the top of the list. He collects his coupon and goes to the car depot. He may have his heart set on a grey model, his wife may wish for a green one. If, on the appointed day, there are only red ones, he has no choice. In the West, the moment a new car leaves the showroom its value drops. In the Soviet Union, the value soars. Because manufacturers meet less than half of the demand, a new car is immediately worth more than twice its factory selling-price, and many of those who buy a new car sell it at once. Even a five-year-old car sells for as much as a new one at the state price.

You do not see in Russia the breakers' yards that in the West are a symbol of motoring plenty and conspicuous consumption. This is no throwaway society. There are 42 cars per 1,000 people, compared with 575 per 1,000 in the United States, and the shortage of vehicles and widespread desire for them ensure that their lives are prolonged. Many people take their cars off the roads in the winter and store them under tarpaulins. Just as fashion-conscious women cultivate a good dressmaker, so the careful motorist cultivates a good motor-mechanic. Such men are prima donnas, used to seeing their customers grovel, and able to command the perks of good meat, vodka and tobacco.

Having bought his car the driver learns to track down spare parts. One bitter January day I heard that there had been trouble outside a car accessories shop. People had formed a queue and hunkered down with typical fortitude to wait all night in sub-zero temperatures. They were not there to buy, but simply to put down their names on the waiting list for new tyres. Not surprisingly, some of those in the line suffered frostbite. In the morning others were injured when a frustrated crowd stormed the shop and broke a window.

There is little choice but to go to the black market where a £70 tyre is marked at £200 and a £40 carburettor at £150. The black market is full of horror stories. A man wanting to sell his car is dazzled by a huge offer. He signs away the car and is given a bag full of money. The buyer's thugs close in and demand the money back. There will be no sympathy or help from the police.

Prudent drivers remove the windscreen wipers when they leave their cars, but there is not much they can do to protect themselves against thieves who lift out the windscreen. Sensible men join the petrol queues early, too, particularly on Fridays when people fill up for the weekend trip to the country. Some people buy stolen petrol on the black market, and many hoard supplies in jerrycans which they keep on the balconies of their flats. It is best not to think of the fire risk.

Learning to drive is laborious and expensive. Many instructors require a bottle of vodka from the pupil before they will get into gear. There is mandatory instruction on the working of the engine. The driving test is conducted by the traffic police and is made easier when the driving instructor tips the police and gets the questions in advance. The police stop a lot of drivers, but much of the time they are not so much interested in enforcement of the law or the safe and free flow of traffic as in supplementing their low income. Many people slip a banknote into their driving licence when they hand it over to a policeman. Some of the Moscow police have taken to flagging down foreigners at night in the expectation of being paid off in dollars or cigarettes: on one occasion they stopped a man who was teetotal and, accusing him of being drunk, tried to extort money from him. In Moscow and other large cities the police are looked down on as vulgar country boys. They are not at all respected, and people snort at the idea of their being of much use in dealing with crime.

★   ★   ★

1. St Basil's Cathedral in Red Square – built as an act of gratitude after the Russian defeat of the Tartars in the sixteenth century.

2. In the heart of Russia photographers set up their stalls and umbrellas . . . and the flag of Russia replaces the Soviet hammer and sickle over the Kremlin.

3. The backbone of Russia. Women like these bear the brunt of the struggle to find enough to eat.

4. Weight watchers. Scales in streets and squares are a common sight. This old man has set up his scales in Tbilisi, capital of Georgia.

5. Few people go out without a shopping bag. You never know when a stall might be set up on the pavement. Here women queue for fruit in Kiev.

6. Almost every commodity is in short supply. Queuing for petrol is a routine chore for motorists. This line of cars is at a garage in Georgia.

7. Fallen idol. The statue of Felix Dzerzhinsky, founder of the Russian secret police, was the first to be toppled in Moscow after the failure of the August 1991 coup.

8. Forty-five below zero. Two Yakut children pause outside their school in a Siberian village.

9. Salute to prehistory. A statue of a mammoth outside the Permafrost Institute in Yakutsk.

10. The scramble for the bus in the coldest city on earth: December in Yakutsk.

11. Masha and Dasha, Siamese twins in Moscow, whose extraordinary spirit shows in their smiles.

12. Shortly after this photograph was taken in Lenin Square in Tbilisi, Lenin's statue was taken down.

13. The main square in Kiev, chief city of the Ukraine. There was a statue of Lenin nearby. It was taken away by popular demand, its face covered in a sheet.

14. A Cossack at a nationalist rally in southern Ukraine salutes national heroes.

15. In the Georgian countryside: women with some of the cherry harvest.

16. Farm workers and their children in Lithuania.

17. Ploughing in Lithuania. Farming methods may be old-fashioned but Lithuania is self-sufficient in food.

18. On the anniversary of the 1989 massacre of Georgians by Soviet troops young men pledge themselves to the cause of independence.

19. Relatives of men and women killed in the massacre in Tbilisi grieve together.

20. Momentous times. Outside the parliament in Riga, capital of Latvia, people hear the declaration of independence after fifty years of Soviet rule.

21. After Soviet troops killed fourteen people in Vilnius, the Lithuanian capital, thousands pinned Soviet badges, medals and cards to a tree of rejection.

When I said I was going to the notorious Riga Market, some of my Russian friends shuddered. Everyone knew of its association with crime and the lurid stories of mugging and vice, of racketeers and prostitutes and confidence tricksters and the shifty 'thimblers' who trap gullible gamblers with a version of 'Find the Lady' played with three thimbles.

The market's remarkable feature is a human channel more than a hundred yards long, created by two lines of people who stand elbow to elbow, each line facing the other, making a funnel about three yards wide. Each person in these lines holds up something for sale: cigarettes, shampoo, cosmetics, stockings, underwear, tins of coffee, packets of tea, pairs of shoes, bars of soap, jumpers, chewing gum and toys. Most of the people with things for sale are women, from teenagers to grandmothers. They stand in their human chain for hours on end, silent, grim and pale, faces anxious and eyes watchful. Through the channel moves a mass of people, shuffle, shuffle, shuffle, and I found that once I had entered the funnel it was impossible to get out until, my feet endlessly trodden on and ribs continuously elbowed, I emerged at the other end like a piece of flotsam.

There were no smiles in this market and people spoke only in whispers and mumbles. Each of the vendors was holding something fairly small, easy to stuff into a pocket or a shopping-bag should the police appear in one of their raids on the black market. There was an undoubted tension, eyes darting, and it struck me as I was drawn along in the jostling, shoving crowd what a place of humiliation this was, another of the indignities heaped upon the people. One woman held up a single lipstick, her neighbour a bottle of cheap perfume, another a bar of soap and another a packet of stockings. People leant over and quietly asked the price and the vendors muttered a response. There was no bargaining. Take it or leave it. Some of the things for sale were foreign, American cigarettes and European cosmetics, but most were Soviet-made. They had leaked out of shops and factories and found their way to the Riga Market with the help of the middle-men, who oil the only part of the Soviet economy that works. No doubt some of the stuff had fallen from the back of the legendary lorry, but one young woman holding up a large packet of tea had acquired it legally. It was part of her entitlement in the consignment of food rations delivered to her factory. She was asking ten times the normal price and looked a little uncomfortable, as if it were the first time she had joined the sellers' line. But she soon sold it, for tea is hard to get in many parts of the country and in some places people have been reduced to drinking watered jam when the tea runs out. I first saw the lines in the Riga Market on a weekday. When I returned at the weekend I was astonished to see that there was not one human channel but several, and each was filled with a slow-moving river of tightly-packed people.

Beyond the drab spectacle was another section of the market, small shops and stalls devoted to selling clothing, mostly denim, a fashion which showed no sign of abating. The prices were breath-taking, considering the average wage, but in such a distorted economy it was hard to make direct comparisons with Western prices. There were ill-made leather jackets costing the equivalent of a year's pay for someone earning the average wage. Tee-shirts with English slogans were popular, even if the words were sometimes misspelled. People pressed their noses to the windows of kiosks selling cassette tapes of Western rock music and cards bearing pictures of half-naked pin-ups in pouting poses. Smaller versions of these were pasted to the fobs of key rings.

Several small kiosks sold shoes at high prices, perhaps the equivalent of two weeks' wages. On the inside of the shoes was the crude pencilled outline around which the insole had been cut with blunt scissors. A Georgian trader said: 'People come here to buy shoes because they cannot find them in the state shops. They don't have much choice.' One of the attractions of the Riga Market is that the sellers ask no questions. In state shops people had to prove they were Moscow residents. Here in the market there were thousands of people from outlying towns. All they needed was money.

The little clothing shops were too small to have changing rooms. When a woman slipped off her dress to try on a new garment an assistant held up a sheet for modesty's sake. But the open-air traders did not have this facility and in the narrow spaces between stalls and kiosks young men and women unabashedly wriggled out of their clothes to insert themselves into stiff pairs of jeans. To keep their feet out of the mud they stood on copies of *Pravda*.

At one o'clock in the morning almost everyone in the vast waiting-rooms of the Kiev station in Moscow had succumbed to fatigue and tedium. They sat contorted by discomfort in the small, tight, red plastic bucket seats the authorities had supplied for their torture. They yawned and snored and shifted this way and that and lay against each other for support, their mouths falling open. On the floor and in every recess and stairwell men and women lay slumped by the score, their children huddled together. They were all so deeply asleep that they were not troubled by the flies crawling busily over their faces and hands. There was a strong, warm, rank human smell, a smell of old damp raincoats. Surly cleaners went to and fro with mops and brooms, flicking close to the sleepers and stirring low growls from them. Policemen walked by with disdainful stares.

Many of these sleeping people were homeless: refugees from the Caucasian troubles, drifters without permits to live in Moscow, gypsies, ex-prisoners and drunks, people who had slipped through the bureaucratic mesh and were without money, a home, a bed, a job. There were scroungers and sleeve-tugging beggars, petty thieves and hard-bitten prostitutes, a world away from their glamorous sisters courting the favours of foreigners in the big hotels for a hundred dollars an hour.

Quite apart from this drifting nocturnal population of the station, there were hundreds of people simply waiting for a train. Some of them had been waiting for many hours, for days, because it was not easy to get tickets. There are plenty of sellers at all the stations, offering tickets at two or three times the official price. If there seem to be no tickets available, people smile a certain smile to the cashier in the ticket office and slip her a ten-rouble note. The daring and desperate get on the train without a ticket and negotiate with the carriage attendant. But many people without the resources to pay black market prices or make deals have no choice but to get a ticket for the next available train and sit down to wait for hours, often through the night. A hotel room would be too expensive. I met an old woman from the Ukraine who told me she had travelled to Moscow to buy her husband a coat for winter but she had been unable to find one, at least at a price she could afford, and she was returning home empty-handed and disappointed. She was sitting in one of the red plastic seats and had another twelve hours to wait.

In the station *Medpunkt*, the medical office, there was a young doctor on duty, Alexei Borodkin:

Frankly, there is not much I can do for people who come in here. As you can see, most of the shelves are empty and I have very little medicine. Most of the people I see are ill because their diet is poor. They are not starving but they are badly nourished and can't fight infections. They have skin diseases and many of them have bad feet. Some have been in fights and have black eyes and broken noses and maybe a stab wound. In winter they get frostbite. Many who come to this place are medically at the end of the road. It's a real jungle. There is a lot of thieving and squabbling among those you can call long-term residents of the station. The police don't know what to do with them. They can't be bothered half the time. Sometimes they become exasperated and throw the drifters and small-time crooks out. They put them on a train and say: 'Don't come back' – but they always do. Where else can they go?

The buffet is expensive, even though the food is not good, and many people can't afford it. They come to see me, pathetic cases, and the best I can do is give them a hot drink or some sugar, but I can't feed everybody. I sometimes let them wash, too, and I look on it as a sort of medical treatment, hygiene. But the smell when they undress is awful. I can't say it's a great job here. It is depressing, but someone has to do it. I come here seven nights a month to supplement my hospital pay. You must know that the medical profession in our country is badly paid.

Every station in Moscow has its population of homeless and pickpockets and people cadging for food and drinks, but the Kiev station isn't the worst. I once worked on the emergency ambulances and we used to see a lot of low life and pick up the pieces and we reckoned that this was one of the better places. The Kazan station is worse. Why don't you drive over and have a look?

In the great halls of the Kazan station an immense portrait of Lenin presided over a spectacle of squalor and discomfort. Here, too, in a ghostly light, people dozed and fidgeted in their excruciating chairs. In a corner there was a heap of sleeping women and their snuffling infants. A swarthy man was keeping guard. They were Armenians, he explained, refugees from the troubles in the Caucasus, the fighting between Azerbaijanis and Armenians. At one of the guichets a woman bought tickets for herself and her two small children and found a chair. She said her train would leave in fifteen hours. Her children did not cry or wriggle or fret. They seemed to absorb the submissive patience of their mother.

The Kazan station is frequented by small groups who come up from dreary towns along the Volga to work in Moscow as robbers, cut-purses and prostitutes under the direction of various Fagins. Some of these gangs rob people of their clothes in quiet lanes, sometimes leaving their victims only their underwear. But the robbers claim a kind of purity. They do not wear the jeans so fashionable among young Soviet people, scorning them as evidence of the decadence that comes from the West. They steal them and sell them. The Fagins encourage boys to train in gyms to be fit for crime.

The buffet was selling hunks of sweating sausage. It looked like dungeon food and people gulped it like hungry prisoners. Around the greasy counter there lurched mumbling and wild-eyed drunks, shifty young men with ravaged gargoyle faces and staring eyes, and people with bent and broken bodies. It seemed like a buffet in the vestibule of Hell.

If hope has a home in Moscow it is the Wedding Palace. Moscow has four and one of them was not far from where I lived, a cream stucco nineteenth-century mansion with spacious rooms. People can save money by having a plain registry office marriage, but for those who want to make a splash the Wedding Palace is the place.

I went to a wedding one morning and waited with the guests in the wedding chamber, the finest room in the mansion, with wood-panelled walls and a floor of gleaming parquet, illuminated by chandeliers. A red carpet ran from the double doors to a heavy magisterial desk. Behind this stood the wedding inspector, a hand-some woman in a long black velvet skirt and white full-sleeved blouse crowned with a Thatcherian coiffure of blonde hair. All the wedding inspectors are women, the administrator had explained to me beforehand, because 'everything done here requires patience and delicacy and men simply don't have those qualities. A wedding is an important occasion and we try to make it happy and memorable. There are many weddings but we try to make couples feel that theirs is special, more than an item on a conveyor belt.'

The bridesmaids and friends clutched posies and bouquets. A six-piece orchestra, with a harpist, pianist and violinists, was ready. A video cameraman and a photographer adjusted their equipment. At a signal the great double doors were flung open and the bride and groom stood framed, looking nervous and awkward. Her cheeks were rosy and she wore a ruched white confection of a dress, slashed to reveal a white-stockinged knee. He wore a blue suit and, perhaps for the first time in his life, a bow-tie.

The orchestra struck up Mendelssohn's 'Wedding March' and the couple walked up the carpet to the desk, stopping at a point where two roses lay. The wedding inspector said a few formal words and the couple and their witnesses signed the register. The sextet played a cheek-to-cheek romantic tune, the sort of thing that night-club crooners sing. A girl attendant stepped forward with the wedding rings and the bride and groom exchanged them and kissed while the pianist serenaded with tinkly sentimental music. From now on, the wedding inspector said to the couple, you are man and wife. The guests scurried forward to kiss and congratulate and the orchestra struck up a happy-ever-after tune.

Outside the cars waited, decorated with ribbons and large linked wedding rings and dolls in bridal gowns. The itinerary was the traditional one for a newly-married couple: Lenin's mausoleum and the tomb of the Unknown Soldier, and a drive to the Lenin Hills to pose for photographs with the panorama of Moscow in the background.

Some weeks before her marriage a bride is given an official card which she presents at a dress shop to order her wedding gown. The card ensures that she will get a ring at a state jewellery store; and she presents it at the hairdresser's to be sure that she is put at the top of the queue.

Hope and dreams have a hard time of it in Russian marriage. Romance often quietly suffocates under the pressure of a succession of abortions in the absence of good-quality contraception, the pressure of poor housing, bad food, queues and cramped accommodation shared for years with in-laws. About half the marriages in Moscow end in divorce. Most divorce cases are brought by women and most of these cite the husband's drunkenness. Soviet sex specialists, a very small tribe indeed, say that ignorance is to be blamed for many unhappy marriages. In strictly repressed Soviet society sex was hedged round by taboos, and discussion and expressions of sexuality emerged only shyly and cautiously as the chains weakened. Stalls were set up in the streets, selling photo-copied manuals of lovemaking techniques and diagrams of coital positions. You could see grandmothers tutting at them or, more often, guffawing. The stalls sold Western nude pin-ups, often roughly copied, and the *Kama Sutra* appeared in Russian cyclo-styled typescript, the pages stapled together like documents from the underground press. There were nude scenes on the stage and on the screen. Inhibitions and restrictions faded as the totalitarian state retreated. When the statue of the secret police chief Dzerzhinsky was toppled, someone daubed on the plinth, 'Sex and Revolution'.

3

DZERZHINSKY SQUARE

When I first went to Moscow I was driven around the city by a Russian. As we entered Dzerzhinsky Square he pointed to the dominating yellow Gothic building on the north-east side. He looked at me and soundlessly mouthed the name KGB, as if it were too dreadful to utter.

Throughout the Soviet period this building, the Lubyanka, was a feared and sinister place and many people shuddered even to be on the pavements outside it. It was the headquarters of the secret police in all its various forms, Cheka, NKVD, NKGB, KGB. It was a bloody bastille, a place of imprisonment, interrogation, torture, murder and execution. It was the evil heart of the apparatus of terror founded by Lenin and enlarged by Stalin and his successors, the operational centre for the long war of repression and suppression conducted against the people. The purpose of this machinery was to defend the Soviet regime and ensure its survival. It undertook the organisation of mass killings, deportations, prison camps, propaganda, censorship, the crushing of religion and of independent thought. Its very size and omnipresence reflected the regime's fear of its own people, and its own uncertainty about its legitimacy. It cast a great net of informers and eavesdroppers over the land, so that people denied privacy communicated by codes, whispers, allusions and meanings-between-the-lines. It was always considered a mistake for a Westerner in Moscow to invite to his dinner-table two Russians who did not know one another, for each would suspect the other of being an informer for the KGB and both would be uneasy and circumspect.

The apparatus was supported by an immense armed force. Quite separate from the KGB border guards and KGB troops, and separate, too, from the Soviet army and its special forces, were the internal troops. This was an army of more than a quarter of a million men. It was operated by the Interior Ministry but was ultimately directed by the KGB. Its purpose was to squash internal uprisings. The size and power of this force was evidence of the Kremlin's concern about the fragility of the empire and its fear of the hatred of its own people.

The offices of the All-Russia Insurance Company on Lubyanka Square were seized in 1917 and made into the headquarters of the Cheka, the political force set up that year to fight enemies of the new regime and to bring people under control by means of terror. Members of the KGB continued to call themselves Chekists in honour of their origins. The Cheka was headed by the fanatical Felix Dzerzhinsky. Robert Bruce Lockhart, who led the British Mission in Moscow in 1918, wrote of Dzerzhinsky's sunken eyes blazing 'with a steady fire of fanaticism. They never twitched. His eyelids seemed paralysed.' The scale of the Cheka murders preyed on even Dzerzhinsky's mind and, drunk at a party one night, he begged others to shoot him. Iron Felix, as he was known, died in 1926 and Lubyanka Square was renamed after him. A bronze statue was raised in the centre of the square in 1958 and the circle on which it stood, amid the swirl of traffic, was forbidden territory because the KGB knew how much their prince had been hated.

The KGB, known in Soviet jargon as 'the organs' or 'the competent organs', oozed along Dzerzhinsky Street, gobbling up buildings and houses and adding new blocks. Nearby in Kuznetsky Street was a building which became a focus, a concentrate, of much of the misery that the Soviet state visited upon its people. This was the secret police reception office. It was just a little guichet set in the wall, and to it came the families of men and women who had been taken from their beds or arrested in the streets. They waited in a long line in the courtyard to hear confirmation that a father or brother had been arrested; but they were never told at which of Moscow's many prisons they were held. They had to journey from gaol to gaol to find out. Many were directed to another guichet not far from the Lubyanka, the office of the military tribunal, and there they heard, in a cruelly snapped response, that the arrested person had been sent to the camps 'without the right to correspondence'. This usually meant a sentence of death.

★   ★   ★

Ada showed me a photograph of herself taken seventy years earlier. I saw a strikingly attractive and vivacious young woman of twenty, with merry eyes and an open smile, shiny cheeks and fine blonde hair. Her forebears were Scandinavians who had settled in St Petersburg. Harry Bostock fell in love with her. He was from Stoke-on-Trent, working at the British trade mission in Moscow in 1924. Ada remembered him clearly as we sat in her little brown burrow, a tiny flat in Moscow decorated with faded photographs and pictures. In her ninety-year-old face and blue eyes a beauty lingered. She was almost blind and asked me to sit beside her on the narrow bed; she reached out to touch my face, the better, she said, to see me. She had spoken hardly a word of English in fifty years.

Dear Harry [she said]. He was invited to teach English to a group of us students. He came to inspect us, saw that there were five good-looking girls in the group and said he would take the job. He was twenty-eight, red-haired and thin and liked Shakespeare. I was enchanted. We fell in love and after a while we were married. He was a wonderful husband and I shall never forget him. He took me to England and we lived there for nearly three years and I became a British subject. I went to college in London to continue my English studies and finished with a first-class diploma. I spoke good English with a London accent and I learnt to ask in the post office, not for 'a two-and-half-pence' stamp but for 'a tuppenny-hapenny'. I played tennis at Hampstead. I was very happy, the wife of a lovely man in a good country. But I grew homesick for Russia. My heart was torn, but I felt I would have to go back. Harry told me he would love me for ever. I returned to Russia in 1927 and I never saw him again.

It took two years to get my citizenship back and then I found a job teaching English at an institute in Moscow. Stalin's wife was one of my students for a while. She came under a different name and dressed in an ordinary way and none of the others knew who she was. She was very shy. Another pupil was Khrushchev, then building his reputation in the party. He stood out in the class because he was one of those country people with an original mind. He spoke very frankly and was not afraid of authority. Some of the well-educated Moscow crowd were snobs and used to laugh at him behind his back because they thought him common, a country bumpkin.

He didn't have much interest in learning English and I can't say he was a good student. He certainly didn't pass his exams. The trouble with Khrushchev was that he couldn't spell and couldn't remember the difference between *b* and *d* in the Latin alphabet. He tried to remember their shapes by putting his hand on his hip and sticking out his elbow, but he could never remember which side he should put his hand on. He was always skipping classes to do party work and his mind was really elsewhere. But he treated me with respect and was friendly and full of humour; and if you heard laughter in the class or corridor you could be sure he was in the middle of it.

Khrushchev, Ada said, always had great faith in the socialist future. A few years later, while he was helping to build this paradise, she became a victim of it. Stalin's secret police smashed her life. On 4 March 1938 they called at the flat in Moscow where she lived with her husband, a professor she had married four years earlier. Those were the years there were so many arrests, so much betrayal, that the cities lay under a pall of fear. The knock on the door struck terror; so, too, did the creaking of the lift in the middle of the night. The NKVD, the secret police, forerunners of the KGB, took Ada to their headquarters in the Lubyanka building on Dzerzhinsky Square.

I was a young woman with everything to live for. I was regarded as a good teacher and I had an idealistic faith in communism. Those of us who were arrested could not understand it. We all believed it was a mistake and that we would soon be set free. It seemed so unreal that we should be accused of being spies or counter-revolutionaries or terrorists.

After questioning in the Lubyanka I was transferred to Butyrka prison for more interrogation. Because I had once been married to an Englishman and had lived abroad, I was accused of being a British spy. In those days it was enough to receive a letter from a friend abroad to be denounced as a spy. My diploma from the London college was confiscated as the document of a suspect. I refused to sign a confession. I said only that I loved my country. I was tried in a few minutes and put with a crowd of others onto a train to Siberia. We were very confused and sad but we still believed there had been a mistake that would be put right.

I worked in the forced-labour camps in Magadan, in the far north. I was made to cut wood. It was hard work and we were always tired and had little time to think. The cold was terrible and you could see your own spittle turn to ice. When the temperature fell to minus fifty centigrade they would not let the horses work and that meant we could not work either. Many people died, of course. In that extreme cold some of them gave themselves an easy death by sitting down and uncovering themselves, taking off their hoods, so that they just drifted away. Women were often more disciplined than men. They would eke out their bread ration throughout the day, giving themselves a tiny nibble to look forward to. The men ate it all at once in the morning and they were driven very hard, starved or worked to death. I grew used to the bitter cold. I do not feel the cold now and I sleep with the window open even in the worst winters.

My husband waited five years for me while I was in the camps and then he married another woman and fathered a child. I did not blame him. He could not know whether I was alive or dead, and many people did not return from the camps. I was in Siberia for nine years and when I came home my husband met me off the train and said he would live with me again as my husband. I loved him and I told him so. I said I would continue to love him but that he could not make me happy by making others unhappy – his wife and child. In any case it would have been impossible: the authorities knew how to torment people, and banned me from living in Moscow. What could he do?

Ada was released in 1947 and worked as a teacher in a village outside Moscow for two years. In 1949 the secret police came for her again in another wave of Stalinist purges. As a former inmate of the gulag she was automatically under suspicion. But this time, instead of being sent to a camp, she was exiled to a central Siberian village,

near a place where Stalin himself had once been exiled as an enemy
of the Tsarist state. She worked as a book-keeper on a collective
farm. Within the village she could move freely but she was warned
that if she stepped outside its boundary she would be shot. Exile was
made bearable because she shared it with a friend, Ariadna Efron, a
survivor of the camps at Vorkuta, in the Arctic, and daughter of
Maria Tsvetayeva, one of the great Russian poets. Boris Pasternak
sent them books. In 1956 Ada was freed, and returned to Moscow.

Reaching into one of the folders in a scruffy suitcase by the bed,
Ada pulled out a sheet of paper. It was a certificate of rehabilitation
issued by a military tribunal in Moscow. It said that the secret police
orders of 1938 and of 1949 which had sent her to the gulag and into
Siberian exile had been 'annulled because of the absence of any
guilt'. Ada was one of the dwindling band of survivors and
witnesses.

> I sometimes feel I am alone on the planet. They killed so many
> good and gifted people. Because I had fallen in love with my
> darling Harry I went to prison camp and into exile for more
> than sixteen years. I did nothing dishonourable in my life and I
> never lied; but in our country our leaders lied and made liars of
> many people.
>
> [She took my hand.] I have the clearest memories of
> England and what I remember about Englishmen is their
> manners. One day, the bus to Hampstead was crowded and I
> had to stand. But there was a schoolboy aged about seven,
> I can see him now, and he stood up and offered me his seat. I
> said: 'But I'm not old.' And he said: 'No, but I am a gentleman
> and you are a lady.' Is good old England still the same?

The skulls themselves bear witness. In the forests of Russia, the
Ukraine and elsewhere they have been unearthed in their
thousands. Usually there is a bullet-hole in each. Stalin ordered the
deaths, and the unquestioning operatives of his slaughtering

machinery faked the charges, rounded up the victims, killed them, and buried them in pits and shallow graves and mine shafts.

In Stalin's thirty-year reign tens of millions of people were imprisoned, enslaved and murdered at his command. It was intended that the bodies should be buried and forgotten. But a phenomenon of the later Gorbachev years was the determined uncovering of the killing-pits and the retrieval of the victims. Their wrists were still tied. Their shattered skulls gave a harrowing human form to numbing statistics.

In 1989 some of the first piles of bones were recovered from a mine shaft near Voronezh in southern Russia, and from them a representative sample of the remains of 350 people was buried with decent ceremony and religious rite in hilltop graves. Clergy and party officials looked on. The occasion was another small step towards the acknowledgement of a terrible truth. A band of people were determined to expose the brutality and enormity of Stalin's war on his own people, whom he hated. There was a strong conviction that until people knew their past – learnt that Lenin, Stalin and their successors had run the country through an apparatus of fear and of lies, that Lenin ordered terror, massacres and concentration camps and that Stalin demanded mass death – they could not begin to understand the present or to understand themselves. Emerging liberals and nationalists made securing the truth of Soviet history the prerequisite of any advance towards democracy. Lies were the ramparts of communist power and privilege. Communists shrank from truth as Dracula from the gleam of dawn.

This search for truth became a significant part of the battle between reformers and hardliners. There were many among Stalin's heirs who resented and stiffly resisted the unfolding of the chapters of horrors. For them the years of Stalin's tyranny represented the age of achievement, of nation-building and heroic ideals and the defeat of backwardness and mighty foes. It was the age of Messianic communism in which Russia found its great historic destiny in the world. It was the age, too, when the communist caliphate created an exclusive enclave of special treatment for itself. Many of the old guard had their feet planted solidly in the past, in the years of ideological certainties, of harsh punishments and deep suspicion of foreigners and of foreign ideas. The truth suggested that their own

beliefs were illusions and that they had been infected by evil and
corroded by falsehood; indeed, the truth suggested that their lives
were worthless and ugly. Thus the Stalinists observed with grim and
troubled eyes the unearthing of bones.

The Kremlin and the official press could not bring themselves to
speak of this mass execution of innocents. In their soothing vocabu-
lary it became 'repression', or the 'blank spots' of history, or
'mistakes'. Many people asked, 'Why rake up the past? What good
will it do?' Stalin's grandson, Yevgeny Djugashvili, a lecturer at the
Moscow Military Academy, said the talk of mass killing was
'propaganda' and added, 'I don't give a damn what people say.
Nobody remembers the judges who prosecuted Napoleon. Only the
Emperor is remembered, and it will be the same with Stalin.'

The movement to discover the burial pits was started by Memorial, a society founded in 1988 to reveal the extent of Stalin's crimes,
to erect monuments to those who died, and to build a library and
museum in their memory. The old guard in the Kremlin were
obstructive, fearing that Memorial would become a powerful vehicle for reformers and nationalists. Memorial ran a competition for
the design of a monument to Stalin's victims and many of the entries
were remarkably moving, even shocking. Many had themes of
suffocation, entombment, crushing and manacling. Some had contorted figures crucified upon a red star. Naked and emaciated bodies
were bound by barbed wire and crushed in agony under blocks of
stone. There was one chilling sculpture of a man with his hands
bound, facing the Kremlin wall. He is seen through a cell doorway,
the view an executioner would have as he approached with his
pistol. One of the exhibits of suffering quoted the words Stalin
uttered at the height of his massacres in 1937: 'Now we live better –
now we live more merrily.'

Stalin died, after a last wild, accusing stare, on 5 March 1953.
Four decades on, his shadow still lies across the land, which is why
some of the artists who exhibited at the Memorial exhibition sent in
their entries anonymously. Almost every family in the land has its
pain, a story of death or sudden uprooting, a father, mother, son or
daughter seized in the night and never seen again. Stalin saw to it
that such suffering was a commonplace, and the tears have seeped
down the generations. This anguish is often plain to see. Old women

clutch faded photographs of husbands or brothers lost in the gulag or the silent forests or the bloody cellars of the Lubyanka. Men and women orphaned as children have no idea who their parents were. One evening in Vilnius I was having dinner at the home of a friend with a Lithuanian and a Georgian who had never met before. The Lithuanian remarked that he had been five when his father was taken, and he had never seen him again. The Georgian said his father had been taken, too, and only lived because Stalin died. The two men suddenly leapt to their feet and embraced, strangers united. 'We are brothers,' the Lithuanian said.

The Soviet Union was largely shaped by Stalin. His institutions remained to shape those who followed him. The Soviet crisis, the ruined land, poor economy and food shortages were a part of his legacy. Stalin unleashed terror to crush people into submission. He destroyed the peasantry by execution, deportation and mass famine, killing off a whole class to institute a new order of collective and state farms to feed huge armies of factory workers who were to make the country a titanic industrial power.

Seeing enemies everywhere, he wiped out every shred of opposition to his absolute power. He destroyed much of the country's leadership, its intellect, its military high command, its industrial and scientific brains. He replaced good and intelligent men with mediocrities and murderers. Few were safe. Anyone with a pen-friend abroad was arrested for having subversive international connections; so were those who knew Esperanto. To force confessions, wives were tortured in front of husbands and daughters raped before the eyes of their fathers. Betrayal was hailed as a virtue, narks honoured. In the 1930s the boy Pavlik Morozov was celebrated as a hero of the new communist morality in which black was called white: he denounced his father to the authorities for anti-Soviet views, and his father was shot.

Deportation, torture and execution took on industrial proportions. In Leningrad blood drained from a prison into the Neva. Stalin set his myrmidons quotas of killing to fulfil. In the years of his purges he signed away lives almost daily. On one day in 1937, he and his aide Molotov signed 3,167 death sentences and then went off to see a film.

We do not know how many Stalin killed. Twenty million,

certainly. Thirty million, maybe. Forty million, perhaps. Stalin was the cruellest of monsters, but it is worth remembering how many people readily became part of his cockroach army, recruited as torturers, gloating prosecutors, tame judges, secret police chiefs, informers, murderers, willing clerks and gaolers. It is worth remembering, too, that Stalin was a convenient scapegoat for those who followed him, that the system of persecution and the rule of fear lived on, that the KGB developed and expanded its inherited apparatus to persecute the people well into the 1980s.

★   ★   ★

Stalin remains revered and honoured in some hearts and some places. A small Stalin Society meets at a house near Tbilisi, the capital of Georgia, to pay homage at a bizarre waxwork of Stalin in his coffin, a shrine to the man and the 'good old days'. In the town of Gori, where Stalin was born in 1879, there is a Stalin museum, a huge Gothic temple which, when I visited it, had been closed for two years: it was too embarrassing for Gorbachev's Kremlin.

The massive wooden door of the museum was shut but a Georgian friend and I gave it a push anyway. It opened reluctantly with a Hammer Films creak and we found ourselves in a purple gloom, the light filtering in from a large, coloured, church-like window at the top of a broad staircase. The place was silent and seemed abandoned, the resort of ghosts, and we felt that only whispers were appropriate. There was a soft footfall. A large, dark, tough-looking young man had followed us in. 'It is forbidden for you to be here,' he said, quietly. We asked if we could look around. 'No – all the rooms are sealed and the doors are locked.' We asked if the building would ever open again and he looked troubled and said: 'Everyone here would like that, but Moscow does not want it.'

Until the museum was closed buses used to bring half a million visitors a year and people stared at the cups and saucers bearing the dictator's image, his leather chair and desk and innumerable photographs. They pondered the bronze death mask. Now the museum is like a remote locked room in a castle where something unspeakable has happened.

Gori, forty miles from Tbilisi, seemed to me a slow-moving and almost lifeless town, pale brown, dry and dusty. Numerous groups of indolent young men hung around. There was little to do and not much to buy. Stalin was a son of Georgia, but he never had any sentiment either for his home town or for the republic. He enthusiastically embraced Russia and never did Georgia or Georgians any favours or paid them any particular respect. But Gori embraces Stalin, terrible warts and all, and sees his achievements as far more important than his crimes.

As well as being the place of his birth, Gori is also the site of his last stand. In the main square there is a bronze statue of him, fifty feet high on its dark granite plinth in front of the pillared mass of the Communist Party headquarters, a building preposterously large for a town of 10,000 people. It is, perhaps, the only place in the country with a statue of Stalin, certainly one as large as this. Thousands of such statues were torn down after Khrushchev's denunciation of him in 1956.

In front of the museum is the restored two-roomed cottage where Stalin, the cobbler's boy, was born. It is protected beneath a marble roof supported by granite pillars and presented as a nativity. When I was there a small crowd of Georgians were having their photographs taken in front of it. Stalin was a Georgian, after all. In Gori, Stalin is all they have. They could not be free of the old monster even if they wanted to be. They are stuck with him.

★   ★   ★

In the late 1980s, the KGB embarked on a cynical attempt to improve its frightening image and to distance itself from its bloody past, to slough its skin. It predictably blamed all excesses on Stalin and his system, and offered to help in the restoring of the good names of victims by attesting to their innocence. It promised to provide, from its immense files, information on the location of burial pits.

The KGB also claimed to be the protector of the people rather than their oppressor. It offered itself as a shield in the fight against crime, as the crusader against 'the mafia', the portmanteau name for black marketeers, racketeers, drug traders and criminals of all kinds. The KGB and the Interior Ministry characterised Soviet crime as an octopus whose tentacles reached threateningly into people's lives. KGB men were cast in the role of good guys.

In traditional Soviet theory, crime grew from capitalism and had no place in the communist Utopia. Crime figures were never published. The state pretended that prostitution did not exist. (Unemployment, too, belonged only to bourgeois societies, and officially no one was out of work.) This all changed with the new openness in the press and the relaxation of certain official attitudes. Crime figures were published, and the statistics and reports confirmed what most people felt, that crime was growing. Newspapers and television programmes reported on a rising murder-rate and prison chiefs said that crime in the gaols was out of control. Restaurateurs paid danegeld to racketeers.

The black market bred crime, of course. It sucked in vast quantities of money and goods, and robbers and shady traders helped to fill the gaps created by shortages. It was said that the black market, the only place where many commodities were available, was used by four-fifths of the people. In hotel bars, prostitutes chatted to foreigners and the dollars they earned fed a network of pimps, administrators, police, doormen and the KGB. To hundreds of girls prostitution was a prestigious occupation and when a newspaper ran a warning article, some girls wrote in to ask how they could take it up. A joke had a young woman hauled before a party committee and asked how it was that a person of her high standard of education, good family background and good credentials could become a prostitute. 'Just lucky, I suppose,' she said. A newspaper noted that prostitutes are not the fallen sisters of an imperfect pre-revolutionary society, but women envied for their beautiful clothes.

I went to see a general in the Interior Ministry and he gave me figures showing an increase in crime. 'There's a moral and spiritual decline in this country,' he said. 'There was a time when a man put on trial was condemned by his neighbours, but today people sympathise with him.'

In any society crime has its tangle of historic, social and economic roots. In the Soviet Union the criminal nature of the state must be added. For many years the country was run by a mass murderer assisted by fanatical secret police chiefs. Moral qualities were attacked and the law was pressed into the service of liars. People were encouraged to be informers. Neighbourliness was corroded. Bribery flourished at every level in the administrative apparatus: it was the only way to get things done. The men who ran the Soviet Union had a vested interest in a system of shortages in which crime and corruption throve. They made the black market a gusher of fabulous profits. Sanctimoniously uttering the platitudes of socialism they robbed and blackmailed the citizenry, embezzled shamelessly, built their luxury villas and lived like potentates with brandy on tap and girls at a finger's snap.

Money was what they ordered up by the sackful to oil the wheels. But what really counted with these lawless lords was power and privilege, the ability to strike fear, to remove enemies, to extort, to demand the golden keys to exclusive shops and clinics and soft jobs and tickets to foreign lands. Gorbachev's ideas of reform and the distant spectre of democracy and a market economy threatened their privileges. The centrally planned economy, with all its inefficiencies, was the source of their profit.

The authorities talked increasingly about organised crime. 'The mafia' was installed in the public mind as a threat. But there was not much evidence of organised crime on any substantial scale, or in the American sense, there was no Soviet Mr Big. The crime figures looked alarming, but there were no statistics available to make historical comparisons and no way of independently verifying them. The drugs problem was small compared with that in parts of the West. And alcohol was at the root of a large amount of crime. It suited the KGB and the Interior Ministry to encourage the idea that master criminals menaced the land, but the fact was that the mafia was embedded in the Soviet system, and its web of patronage and corruption. In essence the mafia was the state, and the state was the mafia.

★   ★   ★

As part of its campaign to rebuild its image the KGB made a video film which depicted the security network as a bunch of selfless family men devoted to the service of the state and society. Subsequently the KGB opened one of its doors in Dzerzhinsky Street, next to the Lubyanka, to admit a group of foreign visitors. In the lobby we examined the notice board of the Central KGB Club. Forthcoming attractions included poetry readings, a rock concert, an evening devoted to the films of Deanna Durbin, the 1930s American star, and a tea-dance. The Evening of Russian Romance had been cancelled.

We were greeted by a man in a brown suit who introduced himself as Lieutenant-Colonel Viktor Rasskazov, a fairly common name meaning story-teller. 'Welcome, dear guests!' he said, with a flourish of his telescopic conductor's baton and a little twitch of his moustache. He said that the KGB Museum which we were about to inspect had been opened in the new spirit of democracy. We set off through brightly-lit rooms filled with display cases, and the colonel's baton pointed out the highlights of KGB history and achievement.

There was a large section devoted to Dzerzhinsky. Looking at his desk telephone, I speculated on the terror he had ordered through this instrument. The museum's coverage of the Stalinist period was scant. Here was one of the famous 'blank spots of history'. The colonel made the point that secret policemen were killed, too, 'in grave violations of socialist legality', and to emphasise his point he switched on a video entitled 'Stalin's Evil Will'. He seemed much more at ease with the KGB's exploits against the Nazis, and the triumphs of the cold war. There was a strange jumble-sale display of captured guns and cipher books and the poison needle that Gary Powers, the shot-down spy plane pilot, did not use. There was a picture of a laughing George Blake and a smiling Kim Philby. There was also Philby's pipe, with teeth marks, and a copy of his book *My Secret Life* inscribed 'To my colleagues in the KGB'.

There were many exhibits which had the look about them of tawdry melodrama, the stuff of bad spy stories: a wig and a bushy Stalin-style moustache said to have been worn by an American spy, hollowed-out spectacle frames, tape recorders and cameras disguised as watches and cigarette lighters, fountain-pen guns and swordsticks. There was also a copy of a once-banned publication, the *Chronicle of the Catholic Church of Lithuania*, a reminder of the KGB's part in the repression of religion.

A little later I went again to Dzerzhinsky Street, by invitation, and was admitted to a waiting-room. An old man in a shabby coat came in to wait, and I wondered if he were an informer here to whisper into ears. The only ornament in the room was a wooden column supporting a white plaster head of the dreaded Dzerzhinsky, which gave a good idea of his unblinking reptilian gaze. At the foot of this idol was a bunch of red paper carnations.

On this occasion the KGB had dreamed up another tasteless prank, in the hope of gaining a little publicity that did not deal with fear and betrayal. A young man wearing a blue denim outfit of the kind much sought after in Moscow came in and introduced himself as Sergei and his young woman companion as 'Miss KGB'. She took my hand and bent her knees prettily in a bobbed curtsy. That she was of the well-fed élite showed in her mane of dark hair, her clear skin and fine teeth. Here was the pretty face of the KGB, but a Soviet newspaper had reported that there was more to her than that. 'Her skill in kicking an enemy's head with her foot', it confided, 'emphasises her maidenly charms.' I wanted to know what a nice girl like this was doing in an organisation with such a terrible history. When I asked her about the KGB's fearsome image Sergei headed the question off, like a good minder, saying that the image had been created abroad. Miss KGB said carefully that one 'never had the feeling that there was something awful about the KGB.'

★   ★   ★

A few days before, a great crowd had moved in dignified silence to Dzerzhinsky Square. In the gathering gloom the people walked down a street in which almost every building was part of the KGB's machine. They were preceded by a van fitted with loudspeakers and as it trundled along someone recited the names of hundreds upon hundreds of victims of the gulag and of the execution squads. They passed the Lubyanka's forbidding granite bulk and congregated in a small garden on the edge of the square. They were there, only fifty yards from the black statue of Dzerzhinsky, to witness the unveiling of a simple monument to the victims of totalitarian terror. There was no need for the KGB to tap telephones or send spies, for the people were at its doorstep. There had never been such a demonstration of public feeling so close to the Lubyanka. People held up placards saying 'KGB – Blood Doesn't Wash Off' and 'Where Is My Son?' Placards were framed with rusty barbed wire. Icons were hoisted on poles along with the once-forbidden flags of pre-revolutionary Russia. A man wore a cap embroidered with his gulag number. After interrogation in the Lubyanka he had been six years in the Arctic camps. The crowd pressed around the memorial. It was a three-ton boulder brought by the Memorial society from Solovki, an island in the far north, in the White Sea. This was the first Soviet prison camp, a place of great cruelty, and was established in Lenin's time, the forerunner of so many.

Perhaps Miss KGB was peeping from behind a curtain as the people in the crowd held up treasured photographs of relatives who were killed or who rotted away in the camps. They held these mementoes, pointing them to the Lubyanka, until their hands were slate-blue with cold. They held them steadfastly as two survivors of the gulag, who had spent more than fifty years in the camps, unveiled the memorial stone. The people did not weep. One sensed that all their tears had been wrung from them long ago.

The demonstration was another of the events that, cumulatively, made what had once seemed unimaginable a possibility. One of the survivors of the camps spoke to the crowd and said that the memorial boulder and Dzerzhinsky's statue were incompatible objects in this square; in my dispatch that night I wrote that 'it is hard to imagine that they will share it for many more years.' In fact, they shared it for only ten more months. Dzerzhinsky was felled and I next saw his statue as it lay on its back in a park, close to a hacked-down red marble Stalin and a lopped-off head of Beria, Stalin's monster. Dzerzhinsky Square became Lubyanka Square again.

4

SIBERIA SQUARE

Among the ghostly silver birches beside the road to Domodedovo airport there stood a concrete staircase. It had been built as one end of a footbridge, but there was no bridge. It was like an allegorical sculpture, suggesting upward progress and the conquest of obstacles, but leading only to a drop into the mud; a plan unfulfilled.

Domodedovo is the principal airport in Moscow for eastern destinations, for Central Asia and Siberia, for the Russian vastness beyond the Urals. It was December and in the gloomy main building there was a brown and grey mass of people, bulky in heavy coats and fur hats, lumbering and shifting like a colony of weary seals. There were spotty pink soldiers in greatcoats of coarse brown cloth and large noisy young men barging through the crowd with their hands full of crude bread rolls stuffed with fatty spam. Impassive black-eyed women from Samarkand and Bukhara guarded bundles tied with string. There were big battered miners with scarred hands and the resentful look of proud men badly used; Caucasian traders foxy in fedoras; flat-faced enigmatic Uzbeks in black caps with silver embroidery. Men and women were packed together, eating, smoking and staring; their children sleeping like puppies, wedged and piled on top of each other.

There were some Armenians bound for Siberia with cardboard boxes containing thousands of fragile carnations. They would sell them for two roubles apiece. Air travel is cheap in the Soviet Union, one reason why aircraft are always full, and people can travel thousands of miles with some suitcases full of oranges or flowers and still make a profit. In the frozen northern wilderness a scarlet bloom raised in Caucasian sunshine carries romance in every petal.

The Aeroflot posters displayed smiling, shapely stewardesses offering comfort and courtesy. My blue ticket promised the same. I carried my bag for 200 yards across the slushy tarmac in driving snow, past the nosewheels of blue and white airliners and into the departure hall. After a while I was rounded up by a brisk stewardess and taken out to join a jostling herd of passengers waiting at the foot of the stairs of an Ilyushin 62. The wings of the aircraft were being de-iced by what looked like a giant's hairdryer mounted on a truck, the nozzle sweeping from side to side. As we waited, growing more pale and numb, an overalled man dragged a brown canvas hose towards us. It emitted a stream of warm dusty air with the smell of an overused vacuum cleaner. Intending to be kind, the man directed it at the plum-faced baby held by a woman standing next to me in the crush. The baby started to cry.

At last the crowd stumbled up the icy staircase, puffing and cursing, like heavily-accoutred medieval soldiers scrambling up a siege tower, the usual disorderly struggle to board a flight. The stewardesses waiting in the entrance looked as if they had opened the door, on a Sunday, to tiresome relatives they had no wish to see. Inside the aircraft there was the familiar dismaying scene. All the surfaces were grubby and finger-smeared. The lighting was dim. People tripped over the wet and ragged carpeting in the aisle and staggered and swore. The rows of seats were jammed close together so that we were packed in like the cargo of a slaver bound for the Indies, knees pressed and numbed against the seat in front. The seats had the distinctive whiff of baby's napkin and some of them fell back drunkenly as soon as they were sat in. Their pockets were silted with old crumbs. Many of the seat-belts would not fasten, and nobody cared. The public address system played loud and discordant pop music. Luggage racks were too small and coats and hats too large and too numerous. The stewardesses soon grew fed up with us. They tried, with mounting irritation and voices rising to a shriek, to sort out ticket muddles, then held up their hands in despair and stomped off waggling bad-tempered bottoms. One of them found a piece of string and tied a flopping chair to the luggage rack overhead to stop it falling onto the passenger behind.

Finally we were wedged in, huffing, sniffing and grumbling, and the door banged shut. We were enveloped in a warm fug, the smell of cabbage and scent and well-worn clothes. The aircraft roared and shuddered down the bumpy runway and we were sucked into the night.

Many of my fellow passengers sat stolidly in their hats and coats, staring ahead like Easter Island statues, neither reading nor dozing, adjusting themselves to the discomfort, enduring their penance. Theirs were faces like those I had seen so often in the long queues, their owners drawing on a patience built into the genes. Not long before, in Leningrad, I had sat on a full aircraft for two and a half hours waiting for take-off. The crew offered no explanation for the delay. The stewardesses said nothing and nobody asked them what was happening, except me, and they were surprised that I asked. There was a problem over baggage loading, I was told. The Russian passengers sat patiently, not fidgeting, requiring no explanation and certainly not expecting one. When I related this later to a Russian friend he said: 'We have grown passive, learnt to wait without complaining. In any case, what difference would it have made if someone had told the passengers what the delay was? Would the plane have left any earlier?'

The Ilyushin flew for six hours. The stewardesses carried a cooked meal to the crew, the smell of hot hamburger and onions lingering teasingly in the air. Some time later, with all the enthusiasm of tired wardresses, they fed the passengers, dishing out trays of grey chicken legs and grey bread with little brown cups of sulphurous mineral water, witches' lemonade. The meal kit included a foil sachet of moist scented tissue which dried as soon as it was exposed to the air. My neighbour roused himself, looked angrily at the chicken and began to gnaw it. I asked him what work he did in Siberia. 'Engineer,' he said gruffly. Did he like Siberia? 'No – I work in Siberia only so that I can get enough money to leave it.' He put down his chicken bone, glared about him for a few seconds and returned morosely to his doze.

We set down in the city of Yakutsk, 3,500 miles from Moscow and in the same time zone as Tokyo. This is the capital of Yakutia, a region of Russia the size of India but with a population of only a million.

'This your first visit?' asked the man in the seat behind me, lagging his neck like a pipe with two turns of his scarf. He grinned a gold-toothed grin. 'Now you will know cold. Real Russian cold, I promise you.'

It was 2 a.m. when we left the aircraft. My face was stung as if by

a sharp slap and I felt my nostrils crackle and freeze. The temperature was around minus forty centigrade. 'Huh – like a sauna here
tonight,' said the golden mouth behind me. 'You're having it easy.' I
soon untied the ear flaps of my fur hat and pulled them down. In
Moscow the demands of machismo oblige many men to keep their
ear flaps up even when the cold is severe: it sometimes seems that
they would rather lose their ears than lose face. But here in Yakutsk
everyone had his ear flaps down.

On the tarmac I was met by a young Yakut woman who took me
to a minibus. After that wearying flight I was enchanted by her
bustling brightness and a smile that wiped away fatigue. In the dark
the road seemed to be a tunnel of ice and snow. All the windows of
the bus were fogged and only through the windscreen was there any
view. We stopped at a smudge of light, the hotel. It was the usual
Soviet sort, grey, concrete and characterless, but the people who
worked in it were rather friendly, as people outside the major cities
often are. My room was much like any other hotel room. It was
small, with a bed not quite long enough, a television set on a
capsizing table and skimpy curtains that did not meet. Although the
window was triple-glazed the room was chilly. I put my overcoat on
the bed for extra warmth.

★   ★   ★

After a few hours' sleep I went down to the small buffet. On a table
beside a fir tree, seasonally decorated with tinsel, my breakfast was
already laid out: hard brown bread, thin slices of cheese and four
boiled eggs. A group of men, one of them a policeman, were having
breakfast. They drank tea from glasses and munched thick wedges
of a sort of Swiss roll, three or four slices each, packing their
stomachs, refuelling. There was nothing else for them to eat except
the boiled eggs which were kept in a large steel saucepan on the
counter.

Suitably egged, I dressed for the outside: thermal underwear, a
thick wool shirt, a quilted shirt, thick trousers, long heavy socks,
insulated boots, a long scarf, thin woollen inner gloves, thick outer

gloves, a fur hat and an ankle-length down coat with a fur collar, like a duvet with sleeves. I went downstairs to the lobby to meet my guide. She was Nadia, a Yakut in her early twenties, rather shy, with a round and slightly solemn face. She had painted her lips with a brilliant scarlet lipstick. She had not met anyone from Britain before. She looked me up and down like a nanny to make sure I had my hat, scarf and gloves, and led the way through the three doors into the startling whiteness.

A century before Kate Marsden, an intrepid English traveller who made an astonishing journey to this region to hunt for a herb that would cure leprosy, noted in her book, *By Sledge and Horseback to Outcast Siberian Lepers:* 'The town of Yakutsk is not a pretty place, and has a dreary, dead appearance.' It is much larger today, but still not pretty.

Yakutsk is the coldest city on earth, and it certainly felt like it. The length and bitterness of winter is the central fact of the existence of its 200,000 people. The temperature drops to minus sixty-five centigrade and people stare into each other's faces to check that their cheeks are not becoming frostbitten. Exhaled breath freezes with an eerie crackling sound. Icy fogs in winter mix with exhaust fumes and human breath to create a suffocating miasma. The schools close when the temperature reaches minus fifty centigrade and lessons are continued on television. At these very low temperatures unalloyed metal becomes brittle. Machines – cranes, for example – have to be made from special steel that does not splinter. Ordinary hammers break when they strike a hard blow. Film splits in the camera, car tyres shatter and pneumatic hoses snap. The ground itself cracks with the sound of a rifle shot. Cars have double-glazed windscreens and unless they can be quartered in heated garages their engines are run day and night so that they do not freeze. Their batteries have to be kept warm. Outside the city vehicles usually travel in convoy because a breakdown could be fatal to a man on his own. He would freeze to death in a short time. All the windows of houses and offices are triple-glazed and walls are fortress-thick with heavy insulation. Buildings are entered through three sets of doors. Milk is stored and delivered in the form of frozen bricks or cylinders with wooden handles embedded in them. Grave-diggers cannot chip at the frozen ground in winter and so they make their mortality estimates and dig enough graves in the brief summer, digging deeply so that the dead remain as well preserved as Lenin. Winter lasts for nearly nine months. The final snowfall is in May and the first in September, often preceded by the frosts of August. Yakutsk stands on the broad river Lena and when the river freezes it is made into a dual carriageway with traffic signs, lights and petrol stations. In summer it is full of barge traffic. Summers are blazing and the temperature reaches almost thirty-seven centigrade. In June and July there is just time to raise crops of potatoes, cabbage and frost-resistant wheat. The summer air is filled with swarms of ferocious mosquitoes which seem to sense that their existence is brief and that they must bite while they may. In the gulag camps in this region gaolers used to punish men by stripping them and leaving them to the attacks of mosquitoes.

The British may talk a lot about the weather, but not half as much as do the people of Yakutsk, for whom temperatures, snow, windchill and thaws are the stuff of life and death. The inhabitants of Yakutia endure the harsh climate of a planet in a science-fiction story.

As we walked from the hotel Nadia said the temperature was around minus forty-five centigrade. The cold snatched my breath away. When I removed a glove to take a photograph my hand grew numb in seconds and ached for some time afterwards. Many people were walking with their faces masked by a scarf or with their mittened hands over their mouths and noses, their heads bent down and eyes red-rimmed. They were anonymous burdened blobs, as fat as bears in their heavy clothes, weighed down by cold and gravity. They stood in huddles at bus stops and rushed the lurching steamed-up buses in waddling herds so that they did not spend one unnecessary second in the cold.

The snow was fine and dry and deep and the distinctive sound of the city was the loud squeaking of trudging boots. At that time of the year, mid-December, the sun appeared, reluctantly, for only four hours a day, hanging low in the sky, like the cold congealed egg of a rejected breakfast. I saw the city only in a thin and milky light or in darkness. In daylight it appeared almost monochromatic, like a blurred old photograph, shades of white upon pale grey, dreary concrete blocks of flats merging into the dirty sheet of mist and dull low cloud. Chalky smoke drifted in clouds from factory chimneys. Billowing plumes of white exhaust rolled and rose in a laboured way. Slow-moving cars, buses and people were floured heavily with snow and Lenin looked incongruously ill-equipped, presiding over the frozen main square dressed only in a suit, with epaulettes of snow. In this vista of unrelieved whiteness and greyness I began to appreciate the shiny scarlet rose of Nadia's lipstick.

The shabby city had its innards showing, like an eviscerated frog in a laboratory. It was criss-crossed by the large pipes and ducts built above ground to carry water and sewage, all of them insulated and heated. Older parts of the city were a bizarre landscape of drowning houses, of buckled buildings with twisted roofs sinking drunkenly and picturesquely into the ground. Some of them were submerged to the sills of their fretworked windows, shipwrecked in the toffee-like swamp of the permafrost.

This is the other main fact of life in this region. All of Yakutia is permafrost, the frozen soil or rock which lies under almost a quarter of the world's land surface and under almost half of Russia and is hundreds, often thousands, of feet deep. But the skin, the active layer as it is known, is only about six feet deep. In summer it thaws and grows soggy and buildings start to sag and sink. In winter, too, the heat from buildings makes the top layer soft. To construct the modern city of Yakutsk, with its nine-storey apartment blocks, its schools and offices with walls a yard thick, engineers have had to come to terms with the permafrost: there is no question of conquering it. They have learnt how to sink concrete piles more than thirty feet into the ground where they are locked solid in the frozen rock. They erect their buildings on the piles, leaving a gap between the ground and the structure through which the wind whistles and helps to ensure that heat is not transmitted.

Modern Yakutsk is a city on stilts. But the system is not infallible. Leaking sewage often damages the permafrost and the piles become like loose teeth in a jaw, so that the buildings they support begin to crack and list. Sewage and chemical waste often combine to cause a kind of cancer in the permafrost which makes the foundations of buildings unstable.

Every visitor to Yakutsk is taken eventually to the city's pride, the Institute of Eternal Frost, or Permafrost Institute. Nina Vasileya who works there and guided me around said: 'Permafrost is actually quite fragile, as easy to damage as glass.' We stopped to talk in a cavern in the pale brown permafrost about forty feet beneath the ground floor of the institute, having reached it through a heavy cellar door. The temperature in the cavern is a constant minus four centigrade.

Recently we lost half of school Number 3 in Yakutsk [Nina said]. There was a leakage of water, the permafrost was damaged and the building just collapsed. We've often told the authorities that the buildings in the city are too close together and generate heat and that there are bound to be collapses. Our advice is that the buildings should be more spread out. But, of course, the authorities don't listen. They argue that there is not enough housing. It's true. Many people here live in terribly cramped conditions and one of the great problems of the city is overcrowding.

I asked Nina what drew people to such a place, where everything seems extreme, expensive, difficult and sometimes dangerous.

I'm not a Siberian by origin. I'm from Kiev. I came here twenty years ago when I married my husband. He's half Yakut. He works with computers. The best part of Siberia is the freedom and the space. The Soviet system is the same all over the country but there is not the same pressure on individuals here. We feel a long way from the centre. My husband loves it, of course. In the winter, every weekend, he goes out at six in the morning and walks twenty miles or so to trap white hares for the pot. In summer we go to the forests and rivers. My daughter who is twenty, and my son who is eight, love the outdoors. Of course, the mosquitoes are terrible and we wear nets over our faces. But not my husband. He doesn't react to the bites. He laughs and says, let them eat!

I have to say, though, that Siberia is changing. When I first came here to live we could get plenty of milk and meat and huge quantities of caviare. Furs were plentiful – and you cannot live here without furs. Now furs are harder to get and there are serious food shortages, a bad business in this climate because we need good food to give us energy. There will be a lot of hardship if we don't have enough to eat. Something else has changed, too. I was never aware of any trouble between Russians and Yakuts, but these days there are some tensions. There is also more crime. Maybe all this has something to do with the shortages which make life more of a struggle.

Leaving the Permafrost Institute I rejoined Nadia. She told me that a third of the people of Yakutia are native Yakuts, many of them trappers, farmers, timber workers, miners, cattlemen and reindeer herders. 'Also,' said Nadia, 'we grow a lot of horses. I love to eat horse. It's my favourite.'

We went back to the hotel for lunch, though we did not have horse. I gave Nadia some American cigarettes. She drew on one and exhaled slowly, her eyes closed, her face a study of bliss. 'Now I feel rich,' she said. Kate Marsden, in 1891, had observed that in Yakutsk, 'All the ladies smoke; and the first thing offered to a guest on his or her arrival is a cigarette.' Russia is one of the world's strongholds of guiltless smoking pleasure, a great solace, and I was never surprised that people rioted in towns where there were tobacco shortages.

The only other people in the dining-room were half a dozen communists from Luxembourg, an official delegation. Nadia eyed them through her luxurious cloud of smoke, noting their expensive sweaters and comfortable figures. 'How easy it must be', she said, 'to be a communist in the West.'

Russians have been in Yakutia since the sixteenth century, when Cossack explorers pushed into Siberia, crushing all resistance. They founded Yakutsk in 1632 as one of the military posts on a long trail blazed by hunters. These men came for furs – red and silver fox, squirrel, lynx, wolf and wolverine. But above all they sought the sable whose lustrous dark brown fur was Russia's greatest source of wealth. Many of the Siberian tribes subdued by these ruthless pioneers had to pay their tributes to the Tsars in the form of sable. Ever since the sixteenth-century reign of Ivan the Awesome, better known as the Terrible, there has been state control of this trade. The sable was known as soft gold, and today a sable coat remains, like an outsize diamond, an ultimate symbol of wealth. The skin of one fine wild sable, most beautiful of the weasels, may cost £5,000 and it may take fifty carefully-matched skins to make one coat. The only place in the world where pelts of the exotic, gleaming Russian sable are sold is St Petersburg. Furs are auctioned three times a year in the Grand Palace of Fur, built for the purpose in 1939 as a permitted chamber of capitalism. When I went there I was shown display rooms filled with tens of thousands of skins hanging on racks. Buyers from Europe and Japan were examining them minutely for colour, consistency and beauty. Around 17 million pelts, four-fifths of the furs produced in Russia, come from farms, but there is still much work for the hunters. Hunting – shooting and trapping – is often part of the traditional existence for the inhabitants of remote regions. They argue that it contributes to the balance of nature. The state licenses more than 10,000 professional hunters, but I was told by the state fur trade organisation that permits are issued on the basis of animal censuses rather than the demands of the market. Furs earn the country more than £30 million a year in foreign currency. But the trade is in decline.

'Look at the empty seats in the auction room,' a British buyer said. 'There was a time when we would be crowded in there. The fur coat isn't what it was. Up to a point it is a victory for the anti-fur lobby in the West. The fur campaign has had an effect, particularly among younger people. You hear of children asking their mothers not to meet them in a fur coat because they would feel embarrassed. But another factor in the decline in sales is that furs are simply not so fashionable. A fur coat is not the status symbol it once was and women no longer aspire to a mink in the way they used to.' Only one fur, I was told, is not affected by the fortunes of the market. The sable retains a special and coveted place, like gold.

Some of the adventurers who opened up the Russian empire kept on going in the spirit of Eastward-ho, conquistadores of the snows. They crossed the Bering Strait, colonised Alaska, where there are still Russian churches, and headed south to California where they made their final punctuation mark at Fort Ross, north of San Francisco. In 1867 the Americans bought Alaska from the Tsar for eight million dollars.

In the nineteenth century Yakutia became a place of banishment, what Maxim Gorky called the 'land of chains and death'. The Yakutsk Museum, founded in 1861 by a political prisoner, has a whipping frame and manacles from that period. But on the whole the penal regime in those days was relatively benign. Under the communists the prison colony became a place of horror, part of the gulag network of labour camps and the final destination, the graveyard, for hundreds of thousands of people.

Yakutia is immensely rich in gold, diamonds, coal, iron ore and oil, a Klondike whose wealth has always dazzled the Kremlin. But it has never been easy money and men have scrabbled desperately for riches they can reach only with exhausting effort. The isolation of life here leads people to refer to the Russia west of the Urals as 'the mainland'. The climate and conditions are worse than in Alaska or the Canadian high north and the physical as well as the financial costs of extracting minerals are very high. Relatively few can stand the conditions for long. The endless dark winters make some people crazy. As in other Arctic regions people fall prey to the cabin fever caused by months of confinement in cold sunless surroundings, made worse by drinking bouts. The pay is good, two or three times the average wage, but the work wears men out and the mines and factories find it difficult to persuade them to stay. The excited and ambitious adventurers who get off the planes in the hope of high rewards are matched by the hollow-eyed veterans in the departure lounge who have found that money is not enough.

Victor Zhuravlev, a journalist in Yakutsk for thirty years, said that the turnover of population is a constant anxiety for managers. 'Half of those who come here go back after one or two years. The higher wages, the climate bonuses and other incentives are not enough. Even those who stay longer don't develop any deep involvement in the region or have any genuine interest. They are here for the money, and that's it.'

I did not talk to anyone in Yakutsk for very long before encountering their resentments. As Victor said, there was a time when there was plenty to eat but now there are shortages. High

wages, long holidays in the Black Sea sunshine and a full refrigerator were once part of the reward for enduring the hardships; but
now Yakutia and many other parts of Siberia have become like the
rest of the Soviet Union, drab, short of food and supporting a
flourishing black market. Flats are as overcrowded as they are
anywhere else and many people live in shabby hostels. People
complain that Moscow takes all the profits from gold, diamonds and
oil and gives very little in return. The tension between Yakutsk and
Moscow is growing.

'People work in the worst conditions in the world,' Victor said.
'They see the diamonds and gold that they dig from the earth sold
for millions of dollars, and then they go into the shops and find
empty shelves. They feel they are not the masters of the riches in
their own land. They have to ask Moscow for food – imagine, they
work in the Siberian winter and have to hold out their hands for
something to eat. It is a matter of shame.'

Victor was right. I went to a café and there was no coffee, only
watery fruit juice. I went to a shop and was talking to a woman
about food shortages when she suddenly cried 'Excuse me!' and
rushed away. With her Russian shopper's eye she had spied a man
bringing in a delivery of apples. Shoppers were onto him like
hounds onto a lame fox. The woman returned, bearing her prize of
two bags of bruised apples. 'Food is the greatest problem of my life,'
she said. 'My two sons are always grumbling that they are not
getting enough to eat.'

So, I said to Victor, what's the attraction? After his thirty years
he is a veteran *Sibiryak*, a Siberian, and is committed to the region.

One word, freedom. I came here from the northern Caucasus,
the area that Gorbachev comes from. I have made my life here
and I love the countryside, the wilderness. In my working life I
write anything I want. I am my own master and feel part of a
growing community. I was talking about this to a doctor friend
of mine and he feels exactly the same way. In his district he is
the only doctor for miles around. He deals with everything,
emergencies, strange diseases, all manner of medical problems. A few years back he returned to Moscow. He took a
good job in a clinic, working from 9 a.m. to 3 p.m., but the

work was limited and he was bored. He couldn't extend himself. So he came back to Yakutia and now he is happy again. He feels needed and useful. I know engineers who have had the same experience. They come here and they can use their skills and their intelligence for the first time. They discover what it is to have pride in a job, to have a sense of responsibility. My son is a journalist here and he is helping to start a newspaper, learning new techniques. He feels he is using his skills. This is a marvellous thing for a person.

This is the exciting part of living in Yakutia. Relationships are stronger, too. I think people are kinder than they are elsewhere. Here, if you see someone lying on the ground you do not pass by as people do in the big cities; you have to do something.

I say this, but I also know that some of the old traditions are already beginning to fade away. There is not the same interest in the land, in going out into the taiga, getting close to nature. People these days watch films on television about the country-side instead of going out into it themselves. They are losing touch. Those of us who know the land worry about the damage that industry does. The machines tear at the topsoil and wreck it and snatch up trees that take a hundred years to grow. We are all greens now, but I wonder if there are enough of us.

The exploitation of Siberia has been rapacious and destructive. Siberian cities are among the most polluted in the country, lying under a pall of dirty air and wallowing in sumps of waste. The landscape has been ravaged. Moscow has made the scrabble for wealth at any cost its priority, ignoring the health of the people and caring nothing for the land, the water and the air.

★　　　★　　　★

Nadia took me to the theatre. We drove in a black Volga saloon, the size of a mammoth, thirty years old and in fine condition, the driver

some distance away from where we sat in the back seat. I felt like a
Politburo potentate.

The theatre was large and modern and we found ourselves in a
crowd in the foyer waiting to check our coats into the cloakroom.
The people were wearing their best. Men were in dark suits, women
in long dresses, party frocks, mini-skirts or fashionable black velvet
shorts with hard-to-get patterned tights. All of them, men and
women, wore stout knee-length boots, made of stripy silver-grey
reindeer hide with a thick felt sole. The boots are expensive, up to
£500 a pair, and they are not available in state stores. They are made
for private sale only. They have been developed over the centuries
and are the best possible footwear for the Yakutian winter.

'They are traditional,' Nadia said, 'and a Yakut doesn't feel like a
Yakut without them.' The people kept their boots on when they
went into the auditorium, and they also kept their hats on their laps.
It is not just that hats are expensive. When the temperature is in the
minus forties or fifties what you wear is a matter of life and death.
Hat-snatching is not a prank but a serious crime. Youths steal hats
from heads in the street and sell them to buy vodka. I was told about
a woman who complained to the police that a sneak-thief took her
coat while she was in the hairdresser's. The police were unsympathetic. 'More fool you,' they said, and gave her a lecture about
the importance of being self-reliant in such a dangerous climate. A
fur is no luxury here. The theatre cloakroom took responsibility for
coats, but not for boots and hats.

The auditorium was almost full. The play was in Yakut and Nadia
translated it breathily into my right ear. It was not too difficult to
follow, for the plot was simple and based on a Yakut legend that she
had already explained to me. In the interval we had a sticky wine
cocktail in the buffet and Nadia had a cigarette, inhaling deeply,
closing her eyes and assuming the expression of bliss I had now
come to expect.

After the play she dropped me off at the hotel and I went to the
restaurant for supper. The restaurant was one of few in the city and
there were policemen at the door in black sheepskin coats and fat
black boots controlling a small crowd agitating and cajoling, trying
to get in. As I climbed the stairs to the dining-room two policemen
were dragging a man down. He had been rendered semi-conscious

by drink and his heels bumped on the stairs as he was helped down. The police were not, I thought, unkindly. They carried the man as solicitous soldiers might help a wounded comrade from the battle-field; and there was, of course, no question of throwing him out into the cold. When I reached the restaurant door there was another policeman sitting on a chair and watching the proceedings, holding a stick across his knees.

I was found a table, and a plate of cold meat and pickled tomatoes was put in front of me. There was the bonus of Hungarian wine. The dining-room was full and extremely noisy and hot, the loud talk punctuated by bursts of uproarious laughter, the air thick with cigarette smoke. The tables were a spectacle of disorder, of plates and bottles of wine and vodka and half-filled glasses. Most of the people were Russians and at every table there was a constant round of toasts and enthusiastic clinking of glasses. A number of red-faced men prowled from table to table like wolves, stopping to slap backs and put their arms round women's shoulders, awarding everyone smacking kisses. Fat men sat back in their chairs easing their belts and contemplating the Rabelaisian scene. Plump women shook like jellies at new jokes. There was at every table a shininess of face and eye.

To everyone's delight the band returned from its break, the musicians set up their electric guitars and other instruments on a low stage and turned the amplifiers to high volume. A tremendous blast of sound made conversation impossible and people leaned closer together to scream into each other's ears. Men and women bounded onto the small wood-block dance floor and flung themselves into action under the coloured lights.

From the corner of my eye I became aware of a woman at a distant table waggling her fingers at me in the way that a crustacean waves its feelers. After a while she advanced towards my table, weaving a zigzag course in her reindeer boots. I knew what was coming. She stood at the table, flushed and bright-eyed, her gash of lipstick slightly smudged, her blonde hair awry. I guessed she might be thirty-nine. She stubbed out her cigarette and reached over and shook my hand. 'Dance with me,' she commanded thickly. It seemed ungentlemanly to refuse. We were swept into the jigging throng and to the pounding music we danced a kind of Yakutian tango, she throwing herself dramatically backwards in my arms, her hair touching the floor. She would not let me go until, at last, when we were half-deaf and fairly exhausted, the band mercifully stopped for another break. My partner returned to her table having first embraced me, aiming a kiss at my lips which landed with all the force of a warm blancmange thrown from a dozen paces. Wined, dined and danced I made my way out of the dining-room and past the policeman, making room for someone else in the knot of people at the door to come in from the cold to enjoy the wild night life of Yakutsk.

★   ★   ★

Next morning I went to one of the most remarkable buildings I have ever seen. A ten-storey hospital was taking shape above the permafrost, a sort of moon city, and the construction of it seemed to me to illustrate perfectly the difficulties that the Russians have in working in this wilderness. The construction also demonstrated to the Russians how much can be done when human relations are considered. This is a particular area of backwardness in the Soviet way of doing things – the official contempt for its principal resource, people.

The hospital is a vital facility and has 150 beds, with another 200 beds in an adjoining hotel to house relatives and patients-in-waiting who have to travel long distances for treatment. It was built as a Soviet–Austrian joint venture. The Austrian manager of the project said: 'People at home thought we were crazy to go ahead with it. The weather and the distances were against us, the logistics a nightmare. Nothing on this scale had ever been attempted before.'

The Russians provided the gravel, sand, steel and timber, hard-weather clothing, boots and hats. The Austrians transported more than 7,000 tons of materials by rail from Europe into Siberia and then 1,400 miles by barge down the river Lena to Yakutsk. In the first part of the project they built a wooden village for the construction workers, with comfortable bedrooms, bathrooms, recreation rooms and a sauna. I toured the village with Nadia and some

Russians. They became very thoughtful. 'All this for workers . . .
Why can't we treat our people like this, like human beings?'

In the first summer of construction the Russians, with their
knowledge of building on permafrost, sank the concrete piles on
which the hospital was to stand. When winter came the piles were
frozen into the ground. The following year, from March until
August, a team of 240 men, Austrians, Czechs, Yugoslavs, Thais
and Russians, worked around the clock to erect the building on the
piles. At these latitudes summer daylight lasts most of the twenty-
four hours and every hour was filled. The first ice appeared in the
middle of August, but a month later, by the time of the first
snowfall, the shell of the building was complete, glazed and sealed,
so that the heating could be turned on and work could continue
inside.

> The most important part of it was to look after the men [the
> Austrian boss said]. We started by recruiting suitable people
> who could stand the strain of living and working in this place.
> It's not for everyone. It is hard and can drive people mad. We
> recognised that it is so rough here that after three months men
> need a holiday. Alcohol was banned on the site and men who
> hit the bottle were sent home. But we turned a blind eye to
> beer-drinking if it was discreet and didn't affect performance.
> We made sure the men lived well and had good quarters and
> food.

He gave us lunch in the canteen. It was a long way from the usual
squalid Soviet cafeteria. Russian and foreign workers sat shoulder
to shoulder over lunches of majestic proportions. 'In the toughest
job in the worst conditions in the world,' the Austrian said, 'we
haven't lost a man or had a single serious accident – and that has a
lot to do with morale.'

One of the Russian managers working on the building said:

> We have learned a lot about our own way of doing things. The
> Soviet system of central planning could not work for a job like
> this. We realised there was nothing for it but to change our
> ideas to get things done. Instead of wasting time on useless talk
> we took action and cut through the red tape. The way this

hospital is being built has opened many eyes in Yakutsk: we are a long way from Moscow, not just in distance but also in attitude. Russian workers compared the terrible conditions in which they usually have to work, with their completely different experience on this job. Here they have been valued. It made them thoughtful.

'It was a beautiful lunch,' said Nadia.

★   ★   ★

Next day we drove out to a village fifteen miles from the city. Its 3,000 people live mostly in single-storey wooden houses and most of them work on a collective farm supplying Yakutsk with milk, pork, cabbage, potatoes and cucumbers grown in hothouses. In the yard or back garden of every house was a large pile of ice blocks cut from those stretches of the Lena river where sewage is not dumped. These blocks were the winter water supply, carried indoors to be melted in a large drum by the kitchen stove.

The wife of a trade union official who showed me her home said: 'Life is not so bad. We are better off in the country than in the town. Many things are rationed but we grow our own vegetables and we have chickens and eggs. We kill pigs in the summer and put the meat into a deep hole in the ground, into the permafrost, so that we have supplies through the winter.'

We made our way to the village store, past a small group of shaggy horses wintering out, the sight of them prompting Nadia again to remark how much she adored horse meat. The shop was like any Russian shop, poorly supplied, with women looking intently at meagre displays of buttons, combs, toothpaste, cheap plastic toys, shirts and a couple of accordions. I peeped over the shoulders of a group gathered around a counter. They were looking longingly at bikinis, blue with yellow spots.

We drove back to the city and I visited the university. As we were leaving we encountered a young couple, she in her bridal gown, he in his best suit. She was Russian and he Yakut. They had just married in the registry office and, both being students, had gone into the university to brush their hair and tidy up before going on to their wedding party. 'It would be good luck to have a foreigner,' they said, 'so why don't you come?'

In a few minutes I found myself in a restaurant filled with a hundred wedding guests. I was installed at the top table next to the bride's mother, with Nadia on my left. 'Wonderful,' said Nadia. 'I hardly ever go to a party.'

The tables were filled with cold meats, chicken, mare's blood sausage, dumplings, pickles, vegetables and salads and bottles of wine, Russian champagne and vodka. The toasts began at once and the newly-weds were called on to stand and kiss each other to a count of eight. An old leathery man sang a Yakut wedding song and more toasts were drunk and the couple stood and kissed again to a count of ten. A man played a sentimental tune on an accordion. There were speeches in praise of the couple's fathers, more songs and more toasts, more kisses, then a song saluting the Yakut troops who won fame in the Second World War for their bravery. A young man twanged a Jew's harp, one of the favourite instruments of the region, so popular that Yakutsk was host to the world Jew's Harp Congress some months later. A flame was lit in a lamp to signify the warmth of hearth and home. More toasts. Just when I thought there might be a respite from the non-stop entertainment a group of young men rushed forward, gently kidnapped the bride and kept her hidden behind a screen at the end of the room until money was raised around the tables for her return.

It was soon my turn to make a toast in halting Russian, at the urging of the guests. 'Very good,' said Nadia loyally. 'I understood every word.' I gave her another packet of cigarettes.

A band struck up 'In the Mood' and everyone rushed to the floor to dance. During a break in the dancing I was surrounded by men demanding to know how they could take part in a market economy. 'Please,' they said, 'tell us how to start joint ventures – we want to go into business.' One young man asked, 'What is your sport?' I thought for a second and said 'Sailing.' 'Huh!' he said. 'My sport is Thailand kick-boxing.' And he leant back and kicked his leg straight out so that his reindeer-boot foot came within two inches of my nose, which everyone thought a good joke.

The eating and toasts resumed, followed by another bout of dancing. At 11 o'clock, when we were all dizzy, buses came to take us away, for in weather that severe no one walks home. The short walk from the restaurant to the bus provided a sobering cold slap. 'Leaving at this time means that you did not see one of our old wedding-party traditions,' said Nadia, 'the fight between young men who have had too much to drink.'

A few hours later she was up to take me to the airport and see me off. I gave her the rest of my American cigarettes and made her a Siberian tobacco baroness. There was a pewtery dawn light all the way to Moscow, matching the pale greyness of the chicken served by the grumpy stomping stewardesses.

5

PETER SQUARE

In Nevsky Prospekt, Leningrad's grand three-mile boulevard, a small black car pulled out of the traffic and the driver agreed to take me to Decembrists' Square. As we rattled along the potholed streets I saw that he was disabled. The clutch mechanism was rigged on the steering column so that it could be operated by hand. The driver said his name was Valery Kravchenko and before long I knew that he was forty-five years old, a musician by profession, that he had a disability pension of eighty-five roubles a month. This is about a third of the average national wage and placed him, along with more than 70 million others, below the generally accepted Soviet poverty line. He worked as a freelance taxi driver three days a week to improve his income and give himself a useful occupation. On the other days of the week, he said, he devoted himself to what he loved best, playing his cello.

We talked for a while about music and about the drama that was gripping everyone's imagination, the struggle for supremacy between the communists who had lost power in the recent city elections and the radicals who had defeated them and who now ran Leningrad. The fact that the city had such strong connections with the Revolution of 1917, and close associations with Lenin, made the communists' defeat especially humiliating and the radicals' victory particularly sweet. The city was a cauldron. There was the sense of an old order being overthrown, a fizzy feeling that anything could happen. Now we'll change everything, people said. Soon Leningrad will be St Petersburg again, you'll see. Rubbish, said the hardliners, that will never be permitted.

Valery was gloomy. He thought the communists were still strong and they had all the money and property and were embedded in the apparatus of government. He said he had good reason to hate the party and started to tell me why, but we reached my destination and had to part company. I wanted to hear the rest of his story so we arranged to meet next day at his home.

His flat, on the third floor of a drab block, was a small comfortable nest he and his wife shared with his father. The entrance hall barely had room for two people to stand. Next to it was a narrow lavatory cubicle and beside that a tiny kitchen hardly larger than a yacht's galley. The sitting-room was filled with a sofa, a table and chairs and a sideboard. A cello hung on a hook on the wall and beside this on a shelf was a display of empty foreign cigarette packets. Such things have a curiosity value in Russia. In the markets small-time traders sell empty Western beer cans for a few kopecks. Valery hauled himself around with the aid of crutches. His wife was at work. 'She's a doctor, gets only 150 roubles a month. She likes the work because she wants to help people, but she's depressed because the clinic doesn't have enough equipment or medicine to do what it should. The situation is made worse because the clinic can't afford to repair its ambulance.'

Valery's father appeared with tea and cakes. He had a strong face and thick grey hair. He listened to our conversation and prompted Valery here and there. He was proud of his son. 'You're sitting with one of the great cellists of Russia,' he said.

As a child Valery studied the cello and showed talent. But at the age of thirteen he was crippled in an accident and his musical career seemed finished. He was confined to his home for two years, hardly able to move. But he persisted with his studies, came to the notice of the cellist Mstislav Rostropovich who encouraged him, and eventually entered the Leningrad Conservatory. He gave solo concerts while he was still a student, and won prizes. After one contest he learned that he had been awarded first prize, but the organisers had given it to another performer because they did not want a public presentation to a disabled man: it would have offended the notion that everything in the Soviet Union was perfect. He flourished, nevertheless, and became a teacher at the Conservatory and a concert performer. He made recordings and gave radio recitals.

His father rummaged in some folders and took out the posters that had advertised Valery's concerts. 'And Benjamin Britten visited him twice,' he said. 'Sat in this room and had tea and listened to Valery playing.'

It was at that time the Communist Party entered Valery's life and set about destroying him. It was because Rostropovich had befriended him. Rostropovich had infuriated the Soviet authorities by giving refuge to Alexander Solzhenitsyn. His concerts were cancelled and his foreign travel stopped. In 1974 he fled the country and four years later was stripped of his Soviet citizenship.

The party ensured that anyone associated with Rostropovich also paid a price [Valery said]. A campaign was started against me and meetings were called at the Conservatory where my personality was discussed. Suddenly the authorities found fault with me. Students were forced to write letters saying that I was unprofessional and that I had been absent when I should have been teaching. It was a campaign of lies and I was eventually dismissed. But I was able to show that these were lies when I appealed to the Ministry of Culture. I was reinstated but the party found other ways to get at me. The Conservatory gave me only two pupils and I had no proper role. I was finished. There were no more concerts or recordings and the invitations to play on the radio dried up. They made me a non-person. The strain of it all made me ill and I didn't play for two years. My parents were appalled. My mother was brought up as a true communist believer and she really did think that communists were the best people in the world and that communism would lead us to paradise. She remembered how she used to shout slogans like 'For Motherland and Stalin'. The persecution was a great blow. It made her thoroughly disillusioned with communism. She went into the party offices and told the officials to their faces that they were fascists.

My experience was not unusual. Many people suffered and were broken after falling foul of the party. It is one of the reasons why so many musicians and artists have gone into exile. I am pessimistic about the future because the party is still strong and I know how it operates.

His father pulled out a bulky old-fashioned tape recorder and began to play a tape of one of Valery's radio recitals. The flat was filled with haunting sound and Valery gazed at the table on which, among the teacups, lay the posters of the concerts he had given as a rising musician, with his name in large blue letters. When I left, the sound of his cello followed me down the staircase.

Valery's father came to show me out and I asked him how his son had been crippled. 'It's a sad story. Valery was at a cottage in the country, a cottage owned by a friend. There was a pistol in a drawer and Valery and his playmates found it. You know what children are like. Valery handled it and it went off. The bullet went through his lung and struck his spine.'

Some months later Valery invited me to dinner. His wife and father had prepared a feast. There were mushrooms picked in the forest, good potatoes from the country, caviare and vodka and wine, a great dish of chicken, another of meat. I knew how hard it was for ordinary Russians to gather the ingredients for such a spread, that behind this meal lay a saga of queuing and foraging. Valery's father refilled my glass and speared another joint of chicken, piling it onto my plate, urging me to have more of the blazing mustard he had prepared himself. I began to say mildly that I had eaten my fill, but he would not hear of it. 'There are still real Russians in Russia,' he said with a sudden and fierce pride. 'The country was robbed by the Bolsheviks and the Communist Party but we've survived. We're still Russian – we haven't forgotten how to be hospitable, how to treat a stranger. When you go back home tell them you met real Russians. Here, have some more chicken . . . pass your glass, it's empty.'

It was, briefly, spring and the city was washed with a fine northern light. In the Decembrists' Square, beside the river Neva, a bride, in keeping with local custom, was placing her wedding bouquet at the base of the huge imperial statue of Peter the Great. The bronze monarch is seated triumphally on a rearing horse atop a massive granite block which is shaped like a rising wave. The rock, weighing 1,600 tons, was dragged and floated in one piece from a village six miles away, an astonishing application of massed muscle which no doubt left a trail of hernias. This was a fitting salute to Peter's memory, for he himself was fiercely and frenetically energetic; a giant of a man, violent, impatient and glaring, striding about and shouting, kicking the lazy dog of Russia to life. Tsar means Caesar, and he was in every inch and pore imperious and autocratic.

Bellowing against backwardness, he sought to haul Russia from its medieval torpor and propel it gasping into the wider and more modern world that he himself had seen and marvelled at. In 1703 he took a bayonet and stabbed it into the ground. 'Here,' he cried, cutting a sod, 'here will be a city.' And, by Peter, there was, and is: St Petersburg, Petrograd, Leningrad and now St Petersburg again. He put tens of thousands of men to work, setting his apoplectic face against the difficulties of building on a flood-prone swamp in an unforgiving northern climate. The city rose in a whirlwind of construction and many men perished in the building of it. By 1712 Peter had his beautiful new capital, a monument to his greatness and obstinacy, a work of art made upon a bog on the Gulf of Finland. He decreed it his bridge to the outside world. He turned Russia's face to the West, to European culture and ideas. Alexander Pushkin, in his great poem *The Bronze Horseman*, inspired by the statue, imagined Peter looking out over the city and saying: 'A window on Europe will we cut through here and, a foothold gaining on this coast, we'll hail the ships of every flag and freely sail these seas . . .'.

The statue is the focus of the plaza that was Peter Square until 1925 when it was renamed Decembrists' Square in honour of the officers who rebelled against the Tsar in December 1825. As a revolution this was the bungled work of bored young men, dilettanti with romantic notions and not much resolve. But at least it was inspired by the ideal of a more liberal constitution; and it fired later revolutionaries.

Peter's city is almost too awesome, too rich. The masterpieces rise shoulder to shoulder, their façades creamy yellow, pink and willow green; and their magnificent interiors house more treasures – paintings, sculpture and furniture. It is as if this bullying, explosive tyrant Peter has bidden you to a feast and ordered you to eat and drink until you reel. You emerge dazed, gorged, hungover on grandeur.

There is a splendid view of the waterfront façades from the deck of the cruiser *Aurora*, starting-gun of the 1917 Revolution, which lies moored by the northern bank of the Neva. Its three straight smoke-stacks and dreadnought bow form one of the best-known icons of the revolutionary period. Along with the hammer and sickle and the face of Lenin, it used to appear every day on the masthead of *Pravda*. On 25 October (7 November in the modern calendar adopted in Russia in 1918) the *Aurora* steamed up the Neva to threaten the Winter Palace, the seat of government. Like the troops in the city's Peter and Paul fortress, the crew of the *Aurora* had gone over to the Bolsheviks. The revolutionaries demanded the government's surrender and when the government refused the *Aurora* fired a blank round. It was a warning and a signal. The Bolsheviks moved on the palace and the intimidated government surrendered.

The city was the capital until 1918 when Lenin reinstated Moscow to its former pre-eminence, a return to the Russian heartland, a retreat from the window on the West. St Petersburg became Leningrad in 1924 but to many of its citizens it was known affectionately, as it always had been and still is, as 'Peter'.

★   ★   ★

Thousands of people were emerging to perform the spring rite of window-cleaning. My heart was almost permanently in my mouth as they stood on sills with buckets and cloths and balanced on parapets like Harold Lloyd. They opened their windows on a new era, utterly different from that on which, at winter's advance, they had closed and sealed them.

The city's communist grandees, overthrown at the elections, were fighting to keep their privileges and property. They were also trying to maintain their hold on the television station, where there was a battle between party functionaries and liberal journalists. Galina Leontieva, a young editor, told me that her paper had severed its links with the party and become independent.

> We've raised the price and for the first time we have to think about money and being businesslike. The party hates it, of

course, but for years I lived with a fear of the KGB and the communist headquarters. They used to call me in and shout and make me afraid. I look back on all that with disgust and I won't be afraid any longer. One thing we have to do is to get more young people interested in politics. Many of those in their twenties are passive and sceptical, a lost generation. A lot of the political energy comes from those over forty who remember the thrill of the Khrushchev thaw and now feel they have one more chance to change things.

In the city hall various tribes of radicals were trying to build a new government from scratch. It was not easy. They had no political experience. They were like men who had never seen a bicycle, suddenly being given a fleet of them; and now they were weaving everywhere and falling off. They had a touching faith in the power of reason to compensate for their lack of experience, but many of them found democracy hard going. They were hurt when the radical press, which they felt should be uncritically on their side, attacked them for their shortcomings. 'Some chaps haven't grown their thick democratic skins yet,' one of the deputies said. 'Free speech is difficult to get used to after seventy years without it.'

The city hall is a palace built in 1839 for the Tsar's daughter, its walls and ceilings painted with nymphs and cherubs and hung with chandeliers and Tsarist emblems. When the communists ruled, the meetings were rigid and the suits dark. The new men were informal: many went tieless and the chairman wore a sweater.

'It's both wonderful and dangerous,' said one of the new members. 'With the communists thrown out there is euphoria, and public expectations are high. But the problems are just as bad and money is short.' Another deputy, an historian, said:

Leningrad has experienced the misfortune of all beautiful imperial capitals – being sacked by barbarians. In this case it was not by Huns but by Russians, by the proletariat and the intelligentsia who consented to its destruction. Like all of Russia and of Europe, Leningrad is living through the collapse of communism. But we should not repeat the mistakes of the Bolsheviks. We mustn't get rid of all the apparatchiks: they know how to run things and we will need administrators.

One of the reasons why Leningraders hated the communists was that the party presided over the deterioration of the streets and buildings of a beloved city. The people had demonstrated their devotion by restoring all the fine buildings damaged in the 900-day siege of 1941–4. The steady decay of parts of the fabric in the 1970s and 1980s filled them with dismay. One of the first acts of the new government was to set up a restoration commission. Valentin Panov, a deputy, was optimistic that the city would be restored.

And not just the buildings [he said]. Many of us yearn to see the city enjoying a revival of culture and manners after the years of brutalisation. For one thing, I hope that our ladies will be returned to us. We have lost our ladies in a certain way, you know. They were ground down and all the hard work drained the tenderness and affection from them. Our children were deprived of their mothers and became hooligans and family life was badly affected. We men would like our women to be restored to complete femininity so that we can become re-sponsible males, better behaved. With the emergence of our ladies from the communist past we can become real gentlemen again.

In Leningrad I often lunched at the Literary Café, on Nevsky Prospekt, for its nineteenth-century atmosphere as much as for the food. It was a state restaurant but was un-Soviet in that there was no sour-faced bully at the door to keep people out and the cloakroom attendant as often as not had a smile. The waiters wore bottle-green tail coats and trousers and open-necked white shirts. They were attentive and polite and could usually find some Georgian wine. The tables had white tablecloths, and flowers. There was always cham-ber music. There might be a pianist accompanying a cellist; or two or three young women in long black dresses playing violins. The first course was a plate of cold meat and smoked fish and then there would be grilled meat and potatoes; and, always, ice-cream. Soviet state restaurants had a bad reputation: they were dirty, sloppy and run by bored oafs. This one was a civilised exception.

I had lunch there one day with Natalya, a friend who worked as a teacher and translator, and afterwards we climbed into a taxi, still laughing at some small joke. 'What have you got to laugh about?' the driver demanded, quickly establishing that I was a foreigner. 'If you lived here you wouldn't be laughing. I tell you, everything in this country stinks. I wish I'd been born in a British colony rather than here. I'm fifty years old and what can I show for it? A wasted life in a rotten country. Well, I have one last hope. My son is in the army in Germany. He's going to desert, defect, make a life in the West. I'll join him, make my escape from this hole. It's the only thing I live for.'

He dropped us off at the Moscow Hotel, where we had arranged to meet Nikolai Yazikov. He was waiting in his battered car, a tall, broad, gangling man of thirty-two with a ready smile. I learnt during our drive out of the city and into the countryside that he was brave, and also a romantic. He was swimming doggedly against the tide: at a time when Soviet agriculture was devastated by the inefficiencies of the system, Nikolai had become a private farmer, facing not only the rigours of life on the land but also the hostility and resentments of people ideologically opposed to private farming. The communists had destroyed the farmers, the kulaks, as class enemies. Kulak was a term of abuse, literally fist but meaning tightfist; and Nikolai had set out to be a modern kulak. Anyone who could was getting away from the land, preferring the relatively better life of the cities. Nikolai had left the security of the city and a job as a driver for a hard life on remote and muddy acres south of Leningrad. We were heading for his farm, the car banging over a narrow rutted lane.

Some of my friends think me mad. Of course, I'm a heretic and communists see me as the thin end of the wedge, but I wanted to be my own boss. I didn't like city life. It's corrupt. I wanted to work the land and grow something, to give my life some meaning. I had a feeling that in the city I would die and leave nothing behind. At least in the country I could plant some trees.

Gorbachev began talking about opening land to private

ownership as a way of improving food supply and I took him at his word. I drove around looking for a house and land and found this place, which was sold to me as a dacha, a weekend cottage. I rented some more land and bought two cows. I knew nothing about farming and I read a book about raising cows. I asked a doctor to show me how to give them injections and I learnt to milk by hand, got the hang of it after a while.

I soon ran into opposition. On the collective farm nearby there were officials who didn't like Gorbachev's ideas and thought that private farming was anti-Soviet. As for the farm workers, they've been smashed down by the system. Many of them believe in nothing except vodka and look on their farm wages as unemployment pay because they hardly have to work. They think I'm crazy to work so hard. They say: 'Okay, you have your patch of land now but tomorrow they'll take it back and send you to Siberia. That's what happens to trouble-makers.'

Some of them are jealous. They give me the cold shoulder and won't even say hello in the morning. They see me as an intruder, as a capitalist. During my first year some of them showed me how they felt: they dumped a load of dead pigs on my land and there was an attempt to burn the cottage down. There was an old woman in the village who threw sticks and stones at me whenever I passed, but one day I gave her a lift in the rain and she stopped throwing things. It is difficult to get repairs done. The last time a couple of electricity workers came out here they were drunk and hopeless so I did the job myself. I tried to get help from the collective farm when the tractor broke down, but they find it hard enough to get mechanics for themselves because the workers are drinking all the time. When I went to the garage to buy some parts I offered them cash and they jeered at me. They said give us vodka, not money. I've seen for myself that the land is a picture of waste and ruin and that the people have lost hope. Some of them blame Stalin, some blame Gorbachev, but I keep telling them they must take some of the blame themselves because they don't want to change things and don't want to work.

Nikolai swung the car off the track and headed across a muddy meadow until we slithered to a stop outside a primitive, patched-up wooden cottage. Nikolai occupied one half of it. His main room was filled by a large home-made wooden bed, two old sofas, two television sets and a table covered with oilcloth. Above the bed hung a picture of John Lennon and on the walls were calendars and, as a pin-up, the cover of a German magazine. The other half of the house was the cowshed, occupied by two cows whose odour permeated the whole building. In the farmyard were chickens and rabbits. Nikolai and his wife made a living selling eggs, sour cream and cheese in the Leningrad market and by raising pigs. But at that time of the year, when the weather was cold, his wife and five-year-old son spent much of their time with relatives in Leningrad. Nikolai said:

It is often hellish here. There are no roads, no police, no doctor. It is hard to find gas for cooking. I have to put up with hostility. Whatever happens in our country, it won't be easy to change things on the land. People have grown used to the inertia, to the obstructiveness and corruption of officials. The party and the managers like things as they are and ordinary people think that life will always be like this. They are not much different from the serfs of the last century; but I think the landlords in the old days were more interested in their serfs than the managers are today.

As you can imagine, there is not much social life around here. The only people who give me their time for a chat are the dachniki, the people who come out from the city to their weekend places, because they are interested in what I am doing and to them I am not an intruder.

It was dark when we set off for Leningrad and the heavy rain was too much for the single inefficient windscreen wiper. The car became bogged down in the muddy field. Nikolai set off into the storm and after fifteen minutes returned with a man who helped to push him from the mire. Both were drenched. 'That fellow has a dacha here,' Nikolai said. 'We talk to each other and I knew he'd help.' He grinned. 'But some people would have been happy to see me sink in the mud, I can tell you.'

★   ★   ★

I found myself in mud again, in a clearing in a forest near Leningrad, watching a re-enactment of a skirmish in the civil war, soldiers of the White army hurling themselves against their brothers in the Bolshevik Red. Cameras were reloaded. So were the rifles. The make-up team daubed gore and debated the merits of Russian film blood compared with British. The film was a life of Boris Pasternak, whose novel *Doctor Zhivago*, set in the cataclysm of the Revolution and civil war and the Stalinist aftermath, implicitly concluded that the post-revolutionary path was a tragic error. Pasternak thought that after Stalin's death it could be published. But as a rejection of totalitarian rule and a celebration of freedom and individuality, it was banned in the Soviet Union. Its publication in the West created a sensation and enraged the Kremlin – a single book made a powerful regime shake with anger. As the work of a writer of such stature it was a blow to Soviet prestige, and the award to Pasternak of the Nobel prize for literature intensified official fury. Pasternak was officially accused of a hostile political act, con-demned as a scabby sheep. The head of the KGB called him a pig. Pasternak's spirit was almost broken and under the threat of exile he was forced to refuse the Nobel prize and write a letter of recantation to *Pravda*, an act which haunted him for the remainder of his life. He died in 1960. He was officially reinstated in 1986 and *Doctor Zhivago* was published for the first time in the Soviet Union in 1988.

Andrei Nekrasov, who was directing the film, told me that he was drawn partly by his own experience to make a film of Pasternak's life. 'The theme of *Doctor Zhivago* is that of a divided nation. In the Revolution some of my own family supported the Bolsheviks and some were on the White side. It is common in Russia to have one half of your heritage hidden. The Bolsheviks tried to create a culture on emptiness, to obliterate what had gone before. Pasternak lived through all this and he felt he had to survive, to depict it all.

Living to tell the story was his destiny, his purpose. After an anguish of hesitation he wrote *Zhivago*.'

Andrei was born in Leningrad and left the Soviet Union at twenty-one after marrying an American student. 'The immediate reason I left was that I would have been called up into the army after university and might have ended up in Afghanistan. The deeper reason was that I felt I was suffocating, that I was half a person. I wanted to experience Western culture. When I worked as a tour guide in Leningrad I met Western youngsters when they came here on their educational cruises. I observed how they behaved, how they spoke so clearly and freely. It had a profound effect on me.'

Later, in Leningrad, I talked to two Russian women whose experiences and opinions put them on opposite sides in the Soviet struggle. Nina Andreyeva, a chemistry teacher of fifty-two, sprang to notoriety as the author of the 'Andreyeva Letter' which first, and most clearly, drew the battle lines between communist hardliners and the budding democrats. It appeared in the hardline newspaper *Soviet Russia* and it defended Stalin's achievements and the idea of the class struggle. Its anti-Semitic tone reflected the prejudices of many in the old guard and it was openly anti-intellectual, anti-parliamentary, anti-Gorbachev. It was intended as a banner to which hardliners would rally against reform and it had the support of Yegor Ligachev, an old-guard Politburo rhino. The Gorbachev camp hit back in *Pravda* and the struggle was out in the open. Nina Andreyeva's watchword was 'Socialism or Death'.

She stood in the doorway of her small flat, a dramatic figure in a red shirt and black trousers, thick brown hair crowning a striking and hawk-like magistrate's face. The flat was crammed with books and documents and bundles of letters – 'letters of support from the Soviet people,' she said, 'from the far west to the far east of Siberia.'

She was voluble and it was hard to get a word in edgeways. She seemed rather pleased to be a hate-figure of the liberals and she expressed a strong admiration for Stalin, whose leadership, she said, had pulled the country from backwardness and built an age of achievement in which people were disciplined and filled with a sense of purpose. Above all, he had made the Soviet Union strong. He had defeated the fascists. She scorned Gorbachev and his 'anti-socialist' reforms, and wanted him out: she stood for a revival of the

Bolshevik spirit. 'The party has lost its way and the country is in a dangerous situation, close to civil war.'

She denied that Stalin was her god. 'Not a god, a genius of political thought and leadership.' And what of the deportations and executions? 'We remember the positive side of Stalin. They were severe times and mistakes were made, but we are not going to cry over them all the time. The same mistakes should not be made in the future. In any case, we have experts who have discovered documents proving that Stalin was not that guilty, that many things are exaggerated, documents showing that these newly-hatched democrats often lie about the repressions.'

When I left she gave me a photograph of herself, and a bag of apples.

Natalia Bekhtereva is a leading researcher in diseases and malfunctions of the brain and nervous system. When she was twelve the secret police arrested her father, a military engineer, and her mother was sent to a labour camp.

I was told my father was in a camp and I waited eagerly for him. I never believed I would not see him again. I saw his arrest as a mistake that would be put right because he was innocent. Everything in our apartment was taken. I dreamed every night that my parents would return and that everything would be as it was. I was only told much later that he had been shot, and as far as I can tell he was buried at a place about thirty kilometres from Leningrad. Only now, in Gorbachev's time, do we have real knowledge of what happened in our history. We never believed it was Stalin who did it. I was sent to a children's home and we used to sing songs about Stalin being the kindest and the wisest.

The director of the home was a wonderful man. He told me that because I was the daughter of a man branded an enemy of the people my only hope was to succeed in my studies, to be first in the school, and he helped me in my struggle to finish school and come first. I feel bitter about what happened in the 1930s, about my father, a kind and brilliant man going down those steps to the basement to be shot, about my mother in the camps for eight years, about the betrayal of our people, about the lie we lived under. What happened was like a plague. Gorbachev's arrival on the scene gave hope. People blame him for many things but he was not pre-programmed. He thought for himself and it was amazing that out of that system there emerged a reformer.

In November 1990, at the parade in Leningrad marking the anniversary of the Revolution, there were no banners of Marx and Lenin hanging from the Winter Palace. There was little enthusiasm for any celebration in the Revolution's cradle. It seemed it must only be a matter of time before the city's name was restored to St Petersburg. Some argued that as the title Hero City was, after all, won for the siege of Leningrad, that name should be retained; but others said it was the city itself they had fought for, not an imposed name.

All of a sudden, as my taxi stopped at a traffic light, two small boys threw themselves onto the bonnet, sprayed the windscreen with soapy water and rubbed vigorously with a cloth. The driver took a philosophical view of the ambush and gave the urchins a few kopecks. 'You see,' he said with a smile, 'the age of free enterprise has arrived in Leningrad.' But for all the buzz about a new economic era, the Soviet decades had left people with no knowledge of what a free market meant, and painfully unfitted to deal with it. There was no clear idea of the value of money, particularly of dollars. When I stopped a taxi and told the driver my destination he said, straight away, 'Twenty-five dollars.' 'Nonsense,' I said. 'Two dollars.' 'Okay,' he said. 'Jump in.' One soon ran into the swamp of inertia: in search of breakfast in my hotel I headed for the cumulus of tobacco smoke at the end of the restaurant beneath which the waiters chatted and lounged. They looked affronted by my approach, the shadow of work falling across their otherwise ordered day.

The city was in ferment, socially and politically. There was excitement, uncertainty, the sense of a storm in the making. There was nervous speculation about what the communists would do to obstruct or sabotage its liberal government, run by the mayor, Anatoly Sobchak. People told me that the old tolerance and patience were vanishing. They spoke of sudden outbursts of violent shouting and swearing in crowded buses – 'It never used to happen.' The food queues were longer than in Moscow and the hospitals and pharmacies had run out of even the simplest medicines, like aspirin. Doctors were asking people to scrounge pills for sick relatives. In a canteen I saw a couple of working men in overalls fall on their sausages and bread, not just hungrily, but like famished wolves.

Peter the Great was dusted with snow and the Neva was frozen when I returned to Leningrad some months later. The dashboard of the cab indicated that Marx and Lenin were not in the forefront of the driver's thinking. Next to the Coca-Cola sticker was a Beatles badge, which was next to a 'Berlin Is Free' sticker, which was next to a picture of a girl wearing nothing but a smile. The Stars and Stripes hung from the choke knob, and the air was filled with the smoke of an American cigarette and the sound of Elvis Presley.

I went to the Walrus Club's cosy wooden hut beside the river to meet Vitaly, the chief walrus. Walruses are people who swim in the river all winter long, hacking holes in the ice to make swimming-pools. I had to admit that all the pink walruses there were a glowing testimonial to their sport, looking rather healthier than the average winter-grey citizen as they skipped across the powdery snow in their swimsuits and bikinis and jumped into the river.

Vitaly said, 'Huh, it's only minus ten. We like to go in when it's minus thirty.' Being a philosophy teacher, he had evolved a theory of walrusism. 'You see, the main difference between a walrus and an average human being is that the walrus has great power of will and is very courageous. He looks for challenges, and needs freezing water as a mountaineer needs mountains. My observation is that the longer you are a walrus the more optimistic you become. I am now sixty-one and I am much more optimistic than I used to be. Of course, many of our friends think we are cuckoo.' One of the walruses insisted on posing for a photograph with me – I in my fur hat, thick coat and gloves, she in her skimpy yellow swimsuit. Vitaly edged into the picture, thrusting his coppery barrel chest into the frame and towards the biting wind. 'Now,' he boomed, 'you see the true spirit of our famous city.'

6
LENIN SQUARE

Andrei was in his middle thirties, greying, divorced, pessimistic, and possessed of a gloomy humour which made him a congenial companion as we walked round Kiev for a day. He took me into a shop off the Kreshchatik, the city's main avenue, and indicated the rotting carrots, battered apples and bad potatoes. 'As you can see,' he said, 'you are now in the fertile Ukraine. You have heard of it, of course. It is famous as the bread-basket of the Soviet Union – that is what all the writers say. They have read our nice guide books. You see these vegetables – as a Westerner you probably think they are poor stuff. Here in Kiev we think of them as high quality, and the people are happy to buy them; and remember, this is a privileged district of the city: here we get only the best.'

He smoked the cigarettes I gave him to the last shred, filter tip and all, until the filter was ash on his lips. Cigarettes were in short supply. We went off in search of coffee and a roll and the first café we tried had no coffee. 'This is a surprise for you,' Andrei said, 'a café with no coffee.' We drew a blank in the next café too, but struck lucky in the third and were served small cups of thick coffee. Andrei was pleased that we had had to hunt for it. 'So now you see something of our lovely life,' he said, smiling through his cigarette smoke.

He did not have a full-time job. He was once a teacher, but someone informed the Communist Party that he had been seen at church services and the party engineered his sacking. He asked me not to publish his full name. 'People say that these days we should not be afraid to speak openly, that things are changing; but the habits made by fear aren't disposed of that easily.'

Andrei was Russian, one of the 22 per cent minority in the Ukrainian population of 53 million. He was sympathetic to the Ukrainian nationalism that was gaining ground.

I have many Ukrainian friends and I understand. They think

their own language is held in contempt and they see Russian as the language of control. This nationalism makes Russians nervous: they dislike change, and freedom has always been associated in their minds with disorder. They have been used to autocratic rulers and believe that democracy leads to trouble. But change must come. Soviet rule has brought the whole country to ruin. It has no human infrastructure. It was created for itself, not for people. The empire has no integrating idea because nobody believes in communism any more; and Gorbachev's reforms have no moral basis because they are meant to extend the life of the party.

Nevertheless, we are hearing voices telling us that things were better when we lived in Brezhnev's kindergarten, when we did as we were told and life was quiet. They are making a seductive case for the army to crack down on the radicals, for a bit of tank therapy.

The Ukraine was the second largest and second richest Soviet republic after Russia itself, and larger than any country in Europe. The rise of a Ukrainian independence movement therefore caused particular alarm in the Kremlin. Without the Ukraine the empire would be significantly reduced, and a heavy weight in the scale balancing the Slavs against the Soviet Muslims would be removed. Gorbachev urged the Slavs of Russia, Ukraine and Byelorussia to stick together. But the Slavic heritage could never be glue enough. Kiev and Moscow have always been rivals, and Ukrainians have never lost their yearning for independence however hard the Russians have tried to squeeze it out of them. Kiev, beside the Dnieper river, was the seat of ancient Russian civilisation and by the eleventh century the greatest political and religious centre of eastern Europe. But Kiev was reduced as the Moscow princes extended their state of Muscovy over all the Russian lands, including territories which had belonged to Kievan rulers. The gathering-in of Russian territories was a Tsarist and then a Soviet policy.

In the 1930s Stalin engineered a famine in the Ukraine to smash farmers' resistance to the collectivisation of agriculture. The secret police and internal troops removed grain and other food and prevented people from leaving their homes to search for something to eat. Six million died. There was, simultaneously, an attack on culture and intellectual life intended to crush the Ukrainian spirit. In 1941 many Ukrainians welcomed the German forces in the hope they would end Soviet rule; and Ukrainian armed resistance to the Russians continued after the war. But the Kremlin stamped on dissidents and co-opted Ukrainian communists to help manage the Soviet machine, making them marcher lords to keep order in their own land.

Not long before I visited Kiev the blue and yellow Ukrainian flag was still banned and the sight of it brought KGB men running, their leather coats flapping. The nationalist phenomenon, in the Ukraine and elsewhere, took the Russians by surprise. An official booklet published in 1983, entitled 'How the Soviet Union Solved the Nationalities Question', declared that 'by unswerving pursuit of the nationalities policy the Soviet Union has solved the problem completely and for good . . . A feeling of being members of one family prevails among the Soviet people.' The booklet, one among tens of thousands churned out by the Kremlin propaganda machine, is a minor memorial to self-delusion. Moscow fostered a folkloric idea of the varied peoples of the Soviet Union and the official literature had pictures of laughing girls and men in embroidered national costumes. But the Kremlin knew that there was more to nationalism that embroidery.

Sergei, an activist in Rukh, the Ukrainian Popular Front, who spent three years in prison for nationalist activities, said to me that 'the Ukraine is the corner-stone of the Soviet empire and without it there can be no empire at all. The problems of the republics cannot be solved within an imperial framework and the Soviet empire must die, as others have. Our task is to help it die peacefully and not in an agonising struggle for life. Seventy years under the communists have not destroyed our soul, but I have to admit that people are afraid of violent change, of taking risks. They want a quiet life or they want to get out.'

Where would they like to go, I asked. Sergei smiled. 'To the United States, of course, to a little house near a big American supermarket. People have such dreams.'

Igor, an earnest student of twenty-three, also had his dream. He hoped to buy his wife cosmetics on the black market. I met him by

chance in the catacombs beneath the Monastery of the Caves where
the mummified remains of monks and abbots lie in glass-topped
coffins illuminated by spluttering candles. Igor was waiting for a
friend who earned money singing in a nearby church, and he had
time to talk. I asked him about food and shortages and he said he
was not worried because his mother worked in a restaurant and was
always able to bring home supplies of pasta. His proudest possessions were the clothes he had on his back. 'They are foreign –
everything I'm wearing I bought in the black market.' Now he was
saving to buy his wife a foreign lipstick. 'She is young and wants to
look nice, but lipstick is expensive.' He confided that he was a little
worried about her. 'She's been searching for something to believe
in. Now she worships Hindu gods.'

For Ukrainians the worst nuclear accident in history, at Chernobyl sixty miles north of Kiev in 1986, was a horrific example, in
their midst, of the complacency and arrogance of the Soviet system,
its fatal corruption. The reactor blew up when a risky experiment
ran out of control in the hands of incompetent men whose bosses in
both Chernobyl and Moscow were equally irresponsible. In a
manner typical of the 'old thinking', the Kremlin and its proconsuls
in Kiev tried to cover up the disaster. Communists have traditionally
buried their mistakes, and they thought they could do so this time.
Everything was late: warnings, information, evacuations, emergency procedures. Equipment, protection and plans for countering the
catastrophe were useless. The episode exposed a contempt for
people, a fundamental malignity in Soviet rule, a remnant of the
Leninist and Stalinist bacillus which had never died.

The existence of huge and vainglorious industrial projects created
without regard for land, air, water and human life is one of the
Soviet empire's terrible and dangerous legacies. When I travelled to
the southern Ukraine I stayed in Zaporozhye, a city polluted by a
thick dusty grey fog from the aluminium smelter. All the time I was
there I had a strong metallic taste on my lips and my nose prickled in
the acrid air. Zaporozhye is only one of many cities where unfiltered
pollutants damage the health of millions. There are many worse
places, not least those built as the Hero Projects of Stalin's years,
where filthy and wasteful factories, their methods half a century out
of date, turn out almost useless products and poison the air for many

miles around. Millions of people exist in the grim tenements beneath the smoke clouds, gasping and diseased and also trapped, for there is nowhere else they can go.

★   ★   ★

It was dark when I arrived in Armenia. With two other correspondents I hitched a lift in a lorry filled with rescue workers bound for the town of Spitak. Half the population of 20,000 had been killed in an earthquake. In the dawn light the town was a panorama of fallen and tottering buildings and gashed roads. Men scrabbled at the rubble with their bare hands, looking for their families. It was December. The newly-found dead lay frozen on stretchers. Coffins, rough planks hurriedly nailed together, were stacked in the streets and heaped in their hundreds on the terraces and around the goal-posts of the football stadium. They were being filled in a continuous procession and carried to the burial ground. A Soviet army officer drove us in his jeep to Leninakan, Armenia's second city, forty-five miles away, and this, too, looked as if it had been bombed. Rescuers stood atop mountains of debris. Pavements and gutters were strewn with shoes, coats and cardigans. Coffins were banked high on every corner and bodies lay under cloths and curtains beside the flattened houses.

The apartment buildings in both Spitak and Leninakan had been badly constructed. I saw how shoddy they were, made of thin, light blocks which crumbled into granules when the earthquake started. People died in such large numbers because the corrupt authorities did not care about building standards and the building materials were inadequate or adulterated. The medical and emergency services were hopelessly ill-equipped. The most effective work was done by teams of rescuers who flew from Britain, France and other countries. People saw how professionally they worked, noted their commitment and compassion, observed the high quality of the tools, equipment and clothing they used. The lesson was not lost. A Russian woman said to me, 'Our government has been shown up for what it is. It doesn't care, it can't cope. All our lives we were taught that foreigners were bad people and now we see them rush to help us. We have been lied to.'

The authorities said that troops had been called in to help with the rescue work. But troops were there, with their rifles and tanks, chiefly because of the stirring of Armenian nationalism and because of the centuries-old feud between Armenians and Azerbaijanis. Even in the aftermath of the earthquake this quarrel remained a fixation for Armenians. More than once I heard mutterings that Azerbaijanis had caused the earthquake with a nuclear explosion. People quickly brought the talk around to the fighting over Nagorno Karabakh, the disputed region inhabited mostly by Armenians which lies within the borders of Azerbaijan. Nagorno Karabakh is a little silk- and wine-making enclave. It has become the focus of a mutual and bloody obsession built on the foundations of ancient suspicions and passionate cousinly rivalry.

I returned to Armenia a year later and was reminded as I drove across the dramatic and rubbled land that, in the wry Armenian story of the creation, God miscalculated while dividing up the world's treasures and when it came to Armenia's turn there was nothing left but rocks. In Leninakan the statue of Lenin, in Lenin Square, sturdier than the flats which collapsed, presided over a city of ruins and shanties. The people despised the authorities for their failure to organise better relief and reconstruction, and said they were condemned to live in their squalid huts for years to come. A young woman some friends and I met took us home to her mother, large and jovial, who insisted on cooking us lunch. We were enveloped in an extraordinary mixture of Armenian warmth and generous hospitality, shot through with suspicion of Azerbaijanis. Eat, eat, said our hostess, ladling second and third helpings while telling us that Gorbachev's name was of Azerbaijani origin and that soon most of the Soviet government would be Muslim; and had we heard that Azerbaijan sent poisoned milk to Armenia?

In Spitak, too, little had been done and people were sitting out winter's harshness in huts and tents. Near the town, in sharp contrast, was a village of prefabricated houses for 2,000 people, shops and schools and a clinic, speedily built with Italian money in the space of a few months. An Italian aid worker said: 'Much of what has been done to help people here has been done by foreigners, not local people. The Soviet authorities begin projects but do not finish them. These people have been robbed of their spirit, partly by the shock of the earthquake, but also by the system under which they live. They have been made passive. But that was a problem before the earthquake.'

In Yerevan, the Armenian capital, the hotel dining-room was closed but the receptionist, faced with a challenge to the country's tradition of hospitality, tracked down a restaurant. After our meal we were summoned to an adjoining room where a noisy birthday dinner was in progress. 'You can come in as long as you don't speak Russian,' an Armenian said with a smile. As an honoured guest I was given a pile of plates to smash onto the floor, adding to the uproar.

At the airport we received the sobering news that there was no aircraft, and no fuel. The waiting-room was seething. The harassed airline staff had no information and put on a special performance of rudeness. We left twenty-three hours late and flew to Georgia to pick up fuel. As we descended into Moscow one of the passengers put on his coat and stood near the exit to be sure to be first off, as if he were on a bus. He stood there during the landing, and no one told him to sit down, because no one cared.

The taxi driver hurtled through the rainstorm into Baku. He twisted his neck to shout at me: 'What country?' 'England,' I replied. 'Ah,' he said, nodding vigorously. 'Margrit Tutcher.'

Mrs Thatcher is the best-known Briton and the best-known woman in the Soviet Union. People like her firmness and vigorous style. They would certainly swap her for Gorbachev or Yeltsin. She made a lasting impression with an appearance on Soviet television in which she dealt roughly with two Soviet interlocutors. In Britain people have been used to seeing journalists gored and tossed by Mrs Thatcher, but in the Soviet Union they had never seen such fun. The second-best-known British woman in the Soviet Union is Samantha Fox, the model, whose image can be seen up and down the country on posters, cards and key-fobs sold in street kiosks and hotel bookstalls.

We splashed past the medieval ramparts of Baku and along the Avenue of Oilworkers, surfing to a halt at the hotel on Lenin Square. The palm trees on the promenade shook furiously in a gale lashing in from the Caspian Sea: Baku is an abbreviation of words meaning windy city. In the morning the wind had died to a breeze and the sea was tranquil and blue. From the hotel balcony I looked out on an oriental city of mosques and minarets, a prize for centuries in the struggles between empires and occupied in its time by Romans, Persians, Arabs, Turks and Russians. Azerbaijan enjoyed a brief independence in 1918, but was easily conquered by the Red Army in 1920.

Oil made Baku. In ancient times it bubbled to the surface and could be dredged up with a bucket. It was the core of the Soviet oil industry and the town was once a forest of derricks. Today the oil rigs stand far out in the Caspian. This natural wealth is a source of grievance, and Azerbaijanis grumble that oil could have made them rich – 'but we have been robbed by Moscow.'

A statue of Lenin bestowed benediction over the vast square that bore his name. At that time much of the tumultuous history of Azerbaijan was being made in that square. Less than a year before, a literary weekly had announced the formation of a Popular Front, and the idea of independence seized the people's imagination. Nationalist rallies of hundreds of thousands filled the square and the Popular Front became a phenomenal political force. Like all Soviet nationalist movements of the late 1980s it expressed resentment of Moscow's rule, but the particular spur in Azerbaijan was the tribal quarrel with Armenia over Nagorno Karabakh, which Azerbaijan wanted to retain as passionately as Armenia desired its acquisition. Gorbachev himself commented sadly that eruptions of old hatred were 'artillery salvoes from the past'. People fled from one republic to the other and many were killed in skirmishes between the two sides. An Azerbaijani said to me, 'I recently met a foreign writer who said that the world thinks Azerbaijanis are barbarians. Is that true? Is that how we seem?'

A few weeks later, in January 1990, the spark fell into the keg. An Azerbaijani mob rampaged through Baku hunting down Armenians and plundering their homes. About sixty Armenians were murdered, but many Azerbaijanis sheltered their Armenian neighbours. Fighting broke out between the two republics and Baku was sealed off by its people, preventing troops from getting in. The Communist Party no longer had a grip on power or on events in the capital. Gorbachev ordered a military assault to restore the city to Moscow's control and to smash the Popular Front. More than a hundred people were killed when the army took Baku. Gorbachev had drawn his line: those who challenged the Kremlin's power would have to reckon with the tanks.

★　　　★　　　★

Georgians, Russians say, rolling their eyes heavenward, Georgians ... well, what do you expect? Russians disapprove of Georgians, and also envy them. Georgians are dark, noisy, quarrelsome, hot-blooded, exuberant, poetic, over-sensitive, famously and extravagantly hospitable, proud, passionate and showy. Compared with most Russians, Georgians know how to live. They eat better, drink, cook and dress better. They smile more. Russians stand in queues: Georgians do not. They sit and drink wine. They have more cars and own more land and more of their wealth is in private hands. They have always thumbed their noses at bureaucrats. In Russian jokes they are cunning, thieving and lusty. Russians mutter about Georgian millionaires and black marketeers flying up to Moscow with suitcases full of expensive oranges and making fat profits from hapless Muscovites while casting their dark eyes over Russian girls. They envy them their Caucasian sunshine and rich land yielding abundant tea, fruit, flowers, walnuts and wine. The hill-country of Kakhetia is the Georgian Bordeaux. Many Georgians have their own small vineyards and, judging by the good red wine I have drunk in Georgia, Georgians keep the best for themselves and send the rough plonk to Moscow.

Most of my recollections of Georgia seem to be attached to the vine and the table. At dinner in Tbilisi one night the waitress said approvingly that the wine we had ordered had been Stalin's favourite. Whether it was true, whether she said it to every foreigner, I cannot say. It helped with the lamb kebabs and with the spinach soaked heavily in the garlic which, Georgians swear, is one reason for their longevity. It was just as well we left some room, for we were later summoned to the home of a scientist for a late supper of caviare, salty cheese, cheesecake, grape-and-walnut sausage, tea and brandy, good red wine and – an assurance of sweet dreams – a dish of rose petals steeped in syrup.

Guests in Georgia are honoured, and are likely to be put under the table with toasts drunk from rams' horns. The best way to insult a Georgian is to try to pick up the bill, or to shrink from draining your glass. Returning one evening from lunch I encountered a friend who had also been out. His lunch had been more spectacular: the table was so heavily laden with food and drink it had collapsed.

Georgians grow up in a society that loves laughing, dancing, drinking, feasting and poetry: but the drinking is not always uproarious and a bottle will be produced, more often than not, as an aid to a long and gentle conversation. Still, I found there was nothing quite like the atmosphere of a bar in Tbilisi. In the early evening the air was hot and thick with smoke, chatter, argument and the smell of beer and wine. Men jostled around the puddled counter and the barmaid kept the beer coming from the tap while the barman sloshed out glasses of wine with one hand and hauled bottles from the refrigerator with the other. You didn't have to speak Georgian to know that what he kept on shouting into the mêlée was that he had only one pair of hands. It was the time of the evening parliament. Men stood at the tall bar-tables munching their snacks and addressing each other as if they were meetings. Every now and then they stared dumbfounded at their empty glasses and then ducked into the ruck around the bar, emerging like scrum-halves with a bottle or two of chilled white wine.

Georgians have swagger and self-esteem. You can see some of their style on Rustaveli Avenue, the main street of Tbilisi, a proper boulevard lined with plane trees and cafés which presents, almost every evening, the spectacle of the Georgian *paseo*. Men, and stylish women in dresses of black, purple, grey and mauve, saunter and stop to gossip. Rustaveli Avenue is where great events happen and where history is made, the beating heart of a city that traces its traditions at least to the fourth century. Tbilisi means 'the town of hot springs' and owes its beginnings to its sulphurous waters and dramatic location above the rushing brown Kura river. It sprawls picturesquely over hillsides intricately veined with steep winding lanes. Secret alleys lead to intriguing courtyards with carved wooden balconies and galleries. Peep into the courtyards and you might spy a Mercedes. Tbilisi has about it something of Turkey, a feeling of Greece, a dash of the Mediterranean and the Middle East, but is, in totality, distinctly Georgian.

There are about four million Georgians and they have a robust sense of themselves and their culture. There is no Georgian diaspora. Their 27,000 square miles of rugged and stubborn land are a rock-pool lodged between the West and the Orient, a Christian kingdom and redoubt on Islam's frontier. This is the land where Jason sought the Golden Fleece and Zeus chained Prometheus. Stout forts rising from Caucasian crags bear witness to a history of invasion. The saga stretches back sixteen centuries, to the first Georgian king. The singular language, which has no relatives, dates at least from the fifth century and its whorly, worm-cast script from the thirteenth century. As keepers of a Christian gateway Georgians have acted in the names of St Elias the Pious and of St Nino, and of such heroes as King David the Builder, King Georgi the Splendid, and Queen Tamara, whose twelfth-century reign was a golden age. Many of the churches that stand today were built during her time and then flourished, too, the greatest of all Georgian poets, Shota Rustaveli. Georgians share with the English their patron saint, St George; and Westerners called them Georgians for their devotion to this saint and others called George.

Within the walls of their mountains and culture Georgians have developed a strong family and community life in which parents are revered and children and grandparents and perhaps aunts and uncles all live under one roof. No one proceeds lonely to his grave: there is always a large crowd for a funeral.

Russians and Georgians alike agree that in many ways the Soviet Union stops at the Georgian frontier. Georgians' pride and their attachment to their culture has enabled them to endure thin times and resist absorption. Georgia was tottering and vulnerable when the Russians took it over in 1800 at the people's request. Its population was only 250,000; but, protected by the Tsarist empire, it began to bloom. In the nineteenth century it was a favourite resort of Russian poets and other writers to whom, with its sunshine, culture, wine and handsome people, it was a version of Italy. In the twentieth century its 150-mile Black Sea coast became a holiday resort, the beaches almost hidden under tightly-packed fried-sausage bodies. The Soviet tourist brochures showed a land of rivers and castles, blue mountains and girls in yellow bikinis splashing in the sparkling sea.

The Communist Party programme of 1961 called nationalism the chief enemy of Soviet rule. Moscow tried to throttle Georgia's individuality and culture but its campaign only had the effect of making the language a focus of discontent. Georgian literature became openly nationalist and there was a strong growth of Georgian cinema and theatre. In 1978, when Eduard Shevardnadze, a Georgian, was the republic's Communist Party leader and Moscow's governor in Tbilisi, the Kremlin tried to have Georgian removed from its position as a state language. Thousands of people demonstrated, forcing Moscow and Shevardnadze to give way. In 1981 there were more anti-Russian protests.

The rise of the Baltic independence movements had a profound impact on Georgia and led directly to the founding of a Popular Front and of other parties opposed to communism. The turning point was the massacre of 9 April 1989, the Moscow hardliners' attempt to crush the nationalist movement by military force: the Stalinist reflex. Thousands of Georgians had been demonstrating for several days in front of the Georgian government building in Rustaveli Avenue with demands for independence. The communist old guard were furious. Three of them – Yegor Ligachev, Viktor Chebrikov the former KGB chief, and Dmitry Yazov the defence minister – ordered troops into Tbilisi and gave authority to General Igor Rodionov, an extreme hardliner, to deal with the demonstrators.

His troops did not use guns. They had canisters of poison gas and sharpened shovels. They waded into the crowd of demonstrators, who were peacefully singing songs and saying prayers and chanting slogans. They hacked twenty to death, mostly women, pursuing them into houses to butcher them. Policemen were injured trying to defend people against the troops. Seven hundred people were wounded and 3,000 treated for gas injuries. The authorities prolonged the suffering of the injured by refusing to tell doctors what the poison was, making it more difficult for them to provide treatment. The official news agency Tass and newspapers like *Pravda* made lying statements about the attack, justifying the hardliners' action. Gorbachev did not give the order for the attack, but he said later that the government had a duty to defend its policy.

Far from intimidating Georgians, this brutality put steel into their resolve to be independent. Grief and outrage became a fuel. The date 9 April was branded into the Georgian psyche and the figure 9 became a symbol. Moscow's failure to admit responsibility for the massacre only increased the sense of grievance. On the first anniversary of the killings the steps of the government building became a shrine and place of pilgrimage. It seemed to me that every flower in the Caucasus had been cut and plucked to be carried here and piled upon the steps. People came in tens of thousands to light candles. Brides placed their bouquets in tribute. Across the road, in a gutter, lay a bronze head of Stalin, battered by hammers. Young men were actively encouraged to ignore their army call-up papers, and more than 100,000 people marched to the Soviet military headquarters behind a banner bearing the single word 'Out!'

The republic was in a ferment of political activity. The talk was all of driving a stake through the Communist Party's evil heart. Political parties were reproducing like amoebas. There were more than a hundred groupings, and even the emerging political leaders confessed they were confused by the jumble of radicals, liberals, moderates, greens – and the inevitable monarchists dreaming of restoring kings and golden groves. Two parties, of opposing views, had named themselves after St Elias the Pious. The nationalist tricolour, which had last fluttered in the years of independence from 1918 to 1921, now flew everywhere.

The Communist Party, so long the home of the ruling class, was discredited: and its collapse threw Georgians increasingly on to their own resources. 'Everyone wants independence,' a teacher said, 'but I'm afraid that if it comes too quickly there will be a terrible power struggle and we could fall into chaos like Romania. Seventy years of communism do not fit a people for instant democracy. Our intellectuals were repressed and there is no democratic tradition, no clear idea of how politics and compromise work.' A film director told me that 'many of these new political groups are like an inexperienced demolition crew. They want to destroy an old house and put something new in its place. But they don't know how much dynamite to use and where to place it. This is a dangerous time.'

Certainly much nonsense was being talked, wrapped up in patriotism and the flag. Some of the new political chieftains strutted around murmuring darkly of plots and ambush, like nineteenth-century brigand princes. The air was filled with petty slanders. The new politics gave life to an old problem, that in this land of distinctive individuality every proud Georgian man saw himself as a chief and not a mere spear-carrier. (In the last century one Georgian man in seven had the status of nobleman.) Egocentricity was one reason why there were so many political groups.

To an outsider, and certainly to the Kremlin, Georgian politics exhibited the makings of a nightmare. The pace of change made the radicals seem powerful. Many of them, intoxicated with the idea of glory to come, claimed credit for advancing the independence movement, and favoured a rush to freedom. Older men urged caution, saying Georgians needed time to learn the political game. But radicals were impatient, and contemptuous of such advice. The young, judging severely, could not pardon their fathers and grand-fathers for tolerating communist rule.

Many Georgians believed that the very qualities which made them different, and Georgia itself unique, would restore them to independence and unity. 'We are a tolerant people,' a man said. 'Jews have always been safe in our land and we have never been hostile to other nationalities and religions.' Raising glasses of wine in toasts to endurance, to Georgia and to independence, they said that Georgians are history's champion survivors. 'Tbilisi has been sacked forty times, and forty times has risen again.'

Others drew comfort from sixteen centuries of history and saw the multiplicity of parties as an unavoidable excess arising from political immaturity. 'We are famous for our polyphonic singing', they assured me, 'in which everyone sings his own part but unites in harmonious melody.'

The choir was a pleasing image, but perhaps the game I went to watch in Tbilisi was a closer reflection of political reality. It was a rough form of polo springing from the warrior tradition and the Georgian love of horses, played with great dash by six players on each side. The ball was picked up in a kind of lacrosse stick and the bareheaded players gave each other a good whacking as they thundered up and down in the dust. In another horseback game, these galloping Georgians threw bamboo lances at each other. I could not follow the rules of either.

★   ★   ★

The flight from Moscow to Samarkand passed over the Aral Sea: there was not much left. What was once the fourth largest mass of inland water in the world is a puddle in a desert of sand and salt and scrub where ships and fishing boats lie weirdly stranded as if someone had abruptly pulled out a plug. The Aral Sea is one of the largest victims of the gigantism of Soviet planners. They plundered it to irrigate the vast cotton fields they ordered to be planted in Uzbekistan, a project meant to make nature bend to Moscow's will. Uzbekistan's farmers once produced more than enough to eat, but Moscow made them concentrate on cotton and turned the republic into an importer of food. The life was choked out of the Aral Sea. Even as it was being drained at a dangerous rate and a new desert was in the making, the planners called for ever more production. Among Uzbeks the fate of the Aral Sea is their most telling indictment of the Kremlin's colonial rule.

After the Crimean war the Russians subjugated Central Asia, taming and humiliating the khans and emirs who had ruled in medieval magnificence and with much cruelty. Resistance was put down with savage slaughter. Samarkand was taken in 1868. In the grand days of the Tsarist empire, and of the communist regime which became the new imperial management, the fabled territories of Central Asia were the jewel in Moscow's crown. Russians took their golden road to Samarkand, to Tashkent and Bukhara, Dushanbe and Alma-Ata, swarming south for the sunshine and the better life, settling in cities older than any in Russia.

For millions of Russians born in the Central Asian republics of Kazakhstan, Uzbekistan, Kirghizia, Tajikistan and Turkmenia, there is no other home. Russia is where father and grandfather came from, a distant root. There are more than 50 million people in Central Asia and about 9.5 million of them are Russians: soldiers, doctors, scientists, engineers, teachers and administrators.

A few years ago, when I first travelled to Samarkand, second city of Uzbekistan, there was not much to trouble the Russians. Nationalist grumbles were muted and there was little sign of any militant Islamic impulse. On scorching days I lost myself in shady bazaars filled with melons and pomegranates and drank cool quince juice and green tea beneath the trees of tea houses where men and women talk and rest for hours. When I returned, the Soviet Union was in the vortex following the abortive coup of August 1991. Communism was collapsing and Uzbekistan had declared its independence. People were stunned by events and fumbling for comprehension. Many of the Russians I met were uncertain, brooding pessimistically, thinking about packing up and heading for Russia.

In some parts of Central Asia an outflow of Russians had already begun, leaving a serious shortage of doctors, managers and other skilled senior people. Thousands bought their tickets out as nationalist feelings emerged and republics raised the status of native languages above that of Russian. Russians began to sense that a strident Islam could gain ground. Anxieties were intensified when fighting broke out between Asian people whose lands had been arbitrarily divided by Russian rulers. There was also feuding over territory between its traditional inhabitants and other occupants forcibly moved there by Stalin.

Declarations of independence in the Asian republics, or demands for greater autonomy, followed by the fall of communism, brought new anxieties for Russians. An immense tract of land bordering on China, Afghanistan, Iran and Turkey slipped suddenly from the centralist grasp. As Central Asians asserted themselves, it was feared that the republics would drift from Moscow's orbit and make closer links with Islamic countries to the south. These people, after all, could have little interest in Gorbachev's concept of a Soviet Union with a place in a 'common European home'. The compass was swinging wildly. Russians worried that it might be difficult to operate a coherent and united foreign policy in co-operation with independent Central Asian republics, that they might take sides in future regional conflicts – for example, between India and Pakistan. Such events might also cause a reaction among Muslim groups living in Russia, such as the Tartars.

Russians feared, too, that the republics might get together to put pressure on their old colonial masters, driving hard bargains for the raw materials that Russians in the past took as of right. Exploitation of mineral and agricultural resources, with most of the revenue going to Moscow and little coming back, sharpened a sense of colonial status. Uzbeks and others found it as easy to direct their anger against the Moscow of the new order as against the Moscow of the communists.

Another cause of grievance was the treatment meted out to Central Asians conscripted into the Soviet army. Thousands of young men, contemptuously referred to by Russians as 'blacks', were beaten, and some were murdered. Many were drafted into the wretched labour battalions, a life of gruelling work. The Soviet army believed that military service would help to mould a Soviet man. They were mistaken. Bad treatment in the services made thousands aware for the first time of their identity. The army, in fact, helped to make nationalists.

Most people in Russia did not know much about their Central Asian possessions, cut off from the rest of the country by deserts, tradition, culture and religion. The republics' demands for recognition raised atavistic fears that the Muslim population would grow large and troublesome, that Islam would fill the vacuum left by the shrivelling of communism. Muslims were a fifth of the old Soviet Union's 285 million population, the second largest group after Russians themselves and the world's fourth largest Muslim community after Indonesia, Pakistan and Bangladesh. The Muslim birth-rate dramatically exceeded that of the Slavs, and in the ten years after 1979 the Muslim population grew by 27 per cent.

Russians form a twelfth of the 20 million people of Uzbekistan. Natasha, a schoolteacher I met in Samarkand, told me she would stay two more years and then go to Russia. Her blue eyes were troubled.

It is not a question of *returning* to Russia – I have never lived there. I was born and brought up in Samarkand and my parents have been here most of their lives and are committed to it. I love this place and my whole life is here. I don't look forward to going to Russia. I hardly know it. I hate Moscow and I think people there are aggressive. So I am caught between two cultures. Life is slower here and more agreeable. There is a joke that illustrates the difference between Uzbeks and Russians: two Uzbeks hear that a friend has had his car stolen, so they agree to organise a collection to buy him another. Two Russians hear that a friend has bought a car and they say: 'Good, let's steal it.'

Increasingly we are looked on as foreigners, and I do not think it will be long before we hear shouts of 'Russians Go Home'. Nationalism cannot be separated from Islam and we are afraid that as nationalism spreads, Islamic feeling will grow.

In order to be able to rule more efficiently the region once known as Turkestan, the communists divided it into four pieces: Uzbekistan, Kirghizia, Tajikistan and Turkmenia. The carve-up left its legacy of quarrels over borders; Tajiks, for example, claim that Samarkand and Bukhara belong to them. The communists began a ruthless campaign against Islam and destroyed and closed thousands of mosques as well as murdering or imprisoning the majority of clerics. Of 26,000 mosques before the 1917 Revolution, only 500 survived into the 1990s. Hostility was fuelled by numerous anti-Islamic pamphlets from the official presses, a tactic continued well into the 1980s, until Gorbachev's liberalisation. But communists always underestimated Islam's strength, and did not understand the extent of its influence in family and clan and tribal life. Islam has been a shaping force in Central Asia from the seventh century, and the Islamic factor is returning to its central importance.

'Of course, Islam never died,' said Imam Haja Rajab Ali. He was serving me green tea, bread and honey at his mosque in Samarkand. 'As the mosques were closed and the imams were killed people prayed at home and in secret groups. Parents kept the faith and passed it on to their children. They observed the fast of Ramadan.

The repressions were terrible, but Muslims accepted them as the will of Allah.'

The previous day the long-closed seminary attached to the Imam's mosque had been reopened to admit sixty students. It was the only theological college in Samarkand, but another was to open shortly. 'There is a heavy demand for places,' the Imam said. 'The shortage of clergy is serious and we cannot keep pace with the revival of Islam – mosques are reopening and people are flocking to them. Not long ago there were only three working mosques in this city. Now there are fifteen, and there will be more.'

He pointed to a man passing by. 'You see him – he is a policeman and a communist but he comes here every day to pray. I would say that a tenth of those who come to this mosque are nominally communists. Even during the bad times, party members wanted religious rituals at funerals.' He said that Uzbekistan's declaration of independence opened the way to direct relationships with other Muslim countries and gave many people the opportunity to fulfil their dearest wish, to make the pilgrimage to Mecca. He did not think that Uzbekistan would drift away from Russia. 'We are neighbours and we need each other.'

An Uzbek lecturer at the university said to me that he was an atheist and regarded the renaissance of Islam as a backward step. 'Some religious people are narrow-minded. But we have to accept that religion is intimately connected with our traditions. We are humble and respectful people, but for all our humility we are dignified and do not want to be under someone else's control. I hope our new relationship with Russia will be good. It will be impossible for us to cut ourselves off completely. We are closely tied economically. I am sorry that so many Russians are leaving; but they fear for their future.'

Uzbekistan said it would keep all the revenue from its gold, oil and gas and would sell its cotton for foreign currency. Following the example of Kazakhstan, it would seek direct foreign investment. 'No need to go through Moscow,' was part of the sales pitch. But the collapse of communism came too swiftly for the Asian republics. They had long lived in the Soviet shadow and needed more time to prepare for life on the outside. The flight of skilled Russians was a reminder of the professional and managerial capabilities Central

Asians lacked; and a reminder, too, that they had been accustomed for generations to being told what to do and how to think, and that now they would have to be responsible for themselves.

The empire's lines of communication were fraying. We boarded the aircraft at Samarkand seven hours late, only to be told there was not enough fuel to get us to Moscow. No one seemed to know what to do. The interior of the plane grew like an oven under the afternoon sun; everyone ran with sweat and babies started howling. Some Georgians started to protest loudly ('Georgians – typical', said the Russians) and there was a scuffle between a passenger and one of the crew. It was no secret that Aeroflot, the state airline, did not have enough aircraft, spares, maintenance capacity and fuel to run efficiently. After a couple of hours some fuel was found and we took off. The aircraft was a flying fruit-and-vegetable store. The Uzbek traders had crammed home-made wooden crates of apples, oranges and peppers into every available crevice and piled melons against the windows and emergency doors. The aircraft filled with a pleasant orchardy smell. The Uzbeks settled as best they could amid their produce, perhaps thinking contentedly of profits to come and dinners at the Uzbekistan Restaurant, not far from where I lived in Moscow. Uzbeks are not natural factory workers. Trading is their talent. They learned it on the Silk Road, long before the Russians came.

7

INDEPENDENCE SQUARE

For the lone traveller on the night train, much depends on chance
and manners. Leaving the clamour of the crowded platform and
entering the two-berth compartment, I would make the acquaintance of my companion for the night. The railways take no account
of the sex of passengers when bookings are made. A tubby snorer
Baltic-bound; a sapphire-eyed princess of the steppe; a pickle-
breathed Siberian describing his life with the aid of cartoons; a
manager with Magnitogorsk's miasma in his lungs; a wolfish black
marketeer filling the gap between our berths with a colour television
set – in such company I had passed many evenings jolting over the
uneven tracks of the Soviet railways. Sometimes, of course, people
had no wish to be companionable; but sometimes we shared picnics
or compared the merits of whisky and vodka and discovered
common ground and shared laughter.

During the first journey I ever made on a Soviet train I met an
official in one of the ministries who was happy to practise his English
in the anonymity of the corridor, and who explained to me that
Gorbachev would fail as a reformer. 'Too many officials, too many
bureaucrats with too much to lose. They'll block him, sabotage his
plans. They have their careers and families to think of, preserving a
way of life which has been good to them. Gorbachev gives more
hope to you Westerners than he does to us Russians. We live and
breathe the system and know how hard it is to change it.'

Boarding the train in Moscow one night I found my companion
already installed, a woman sitting on the edge of her bunk as if in a
chapel pew, her back straight, her book held in front of her like a
shield, an attitude of studious rectitude. She was in her mid thirties,
dressed in black, her fair hair drawn back severely from her
colourless, bespectacled face. She seemed the image of a prim
governess. I closed the compartment door to shut out the noise of

the station, and she gave a brief disapproving acknowledgement of my murmured 'Good evening'.

The train set off punctually, as Soviet trains usually do, and lurched westwards through the gathering dusk. The carriage attendant brought glasses of tea from her samovar. After a while the governess set aside her book and left the compartment, clutching a large bag. Twenty minutes later the door opened and she stood there, dramatically framed and utterly transformed. There was a click of high heels and the silky flash of tight peacock blue trousers. On the bosom of her fluffy white sweater were red satin triangles edged with sequins. He spectacles were absent. Her cheeks were bright with red clown spots, her lipstick was luscious and her eyelids vamp green. Her hair was loose and hung to her shoulders. Her perfume preceded her and struck me like tear-gas. She took up her book but it now looked out of place in scarlet-tipped fingers that should have been playing with the cherry in a cocktail glass.

The door suddenly flew open and a man sprang in like Errol Flynn. His black hair was greying at the temples and his merry laugh held the promise of mischief. The governess threw aside her book and the Russian musketeer urged her to join him and his companions nearby. She took his outstretched courtier's hand and left with a giggle and a clatter of heels. Overcome by her perfume and the rhythm of the train I stretched out and slept.

I jerked awake as the door flew open and the lights snapped on. It was two o'clock in the morning. The governess, burbling and in disarray, fell headlong onto her bunk. She was followed by two laughing men. One toppled back onto my shins. Trying to insert the governess into bed, the fumbling pair reduced the bedclothes to a mere tangle of laundry. Into this uproar stepped the carriage attendant, a picture of blue-uniformed outrage. She angrily pushed the men out, helping each one on his way with a full-back's kick to the behind. She apologised to me, shot my companion a freezing frown and closed the door. The governess lay shipwrecked upon the shore of her bunk. The perfume had staled. I switched off the lights. For some minutes the governess whimpered and groaned and then she bolted from the compartment. She returned and groaned a little more, left again, returned and subsided, breaking wind with a loud report. After this Last Post her low snores merged with the thrum of the wheels.

In the morning we were awoken by a detonation of the pop music that, in Soviet trains, blasts away sleep. In Muslim regions, readings from the Koran provide a gentler shoehorn into the day. The governess lay, her bottom in the air, embracing her pillow. She then gathered herself up and went off to the lavatory's penitentiary dankness while I dressed and drank the tea brought from the samovar and watched the yellow sunlight flickering through the silver trees. The governess reappeared. She wore her black high-necked dress and her hair was drawn back from her pale, bespectacled face. She nodded acknowledgement of my 'Good morning' and sat straight-backed, reading her book virtuously until, fourteen hours out of Moscow and the night consigned to memory, we drew into the brightness of Tallinn, capital of the smallest republic of the Soviet Union.

★   ★   ★

I had not been to Tallinn before, but it was familiar. I knew its crooked, cobbled streets, cone-roofed towers and picturesque gables. I knew them from illustrations in childhood books of knightly legends and wimpled princesses. The medieval quarters of the city, framed by stone ramparts and pierced by steep, narrow, tangled lanes, spoke of doublets and dwarves and the tale of Rumpelstiltskin. Thick towers stood guard, loyal old retainers with affectionate nicknames like Fat Margaret and Tall Hermann. Besiegers' cannon-balls were still lodged in their noble walls. From the high battlements Estonians could look out on a grand view of their handsome city, over red roofs and steeples and scores of weather-vanes. In the Soviet years they gazed longingly out to the cobalt Baltic and beyond.

The city was itself a powerful symbol of endurance anchoring Estonians to their history, and after Moscow I found it a refreshing counterpoint, shaped to a human scale. My hotel was full of Finns who had arrived in raiding-parties on the ferries from Helsinki, fifty miles across the Gulf of Finland. Drink was cheaper here than at home and with their currency Finns could be princes for a night. The Estonians did not mind their carousing too much. 'We have a lot to thank them for,' people said. 'They are an inspiration, the sort of society we could be. They stood up to the Russians in 1940.' Finland was Estonia's window to the West, a strand of hope. Finnish and Estonian are cousinly languages, and Estonians watched uncensored news and British and American programmes from Helsinki. Once, when word went around that Finnish television was to show the erotic film *Emanuelle*, hundreds of Leningraders found urgent reasons to visit Estonian friends.

Estonians gave hours of their time to guide me patiently through Tallinn and their history. Fresh from Moscow, I worried at first that they spoke too freely, but I soon discovered that their frankness was neither bravado nor carelessness. Estonia was on the hem of the Soviet coat, and it was plain that the thread was unravelling. Those were the early years of Gorbachev and people were stirring, gingerly savouring the freedom which was seeping into their lives. They believed that a significant moment in their history had arrived, and that they should grasp it.

'Put your watch back one hour,' said Peter, who worked for the government and took the morning off to be my guide. 'You are now on Estonian Standard Time. Look at the clocks. This is normal.'

He kept saying 'This is normal' whenever he described a new manifestation of Estonian spirit. It was a comforting mantra. He indicated the enamel lapel-badges in the blue, black and white Estonian national colours – 'This is normal.'

Not long before, the wearing of such emblems had been punishable. The national flag was banned when Soviet troops seized the country in 1940. Now there were blue, black and white ribbons artfully arranged in shop windows and tricolour stickers for sale in newspaper kiosks. A man stood on a street corner holding an Estonian flag and talking to a small group of people while two policemen walked by. 'He is talking about independence,' Peter said. 'This is normal.' People had kept old flags hidden in their attics and were now bringing them out. Women pressed the faded fabric to their cheeks.

In the streets, in the air, there was a sense of something extraordinary happening. People seemed to be pinching themselves to be sure they were not dreaming. They flocked to newspaper stalls when the latest editions were delivered. They were players in their own drama. Their homes fell silent and they were all attention when the evening news started on television, because the news was about themselves.

★   ★   ★

The condition of the Soviet Union when Gorbachev took power in 1985 contained the seed of this developing drama. Khrushchev had boasted in the 1950s that the Soviet Union and its socialist machine would outstrip the West and bury capitalism. This was the great contest, the ideological heart of the cold war. But all the remarkable advances in Soviet industry and agriculture were seriously flawed. Production was in the hands of a heavyweight bureaucracy working to ideological plans which barely touched reality or the needs of the population. Factories were scattered over the country without any coherent strategy, so that nuts, bolts, filters, electrical components, valves and gears were made in widely separated plants and brought to inefficient places of assembly along tortuous and mismanaged lines of supply. Agriculture was limited by latitude and lassitude. Doctrine directed the plough. Manufacturing and farming were undermined by poor transport and distribution, by a gross waste of energy and raw materials. There was no serious insistence on economic efficiency. Development was hamstrung by the fetishist secrecy of an apparatus which discouraged discussion and the flow of ideas, retained a monopoly of information, and posted KGB guards over photocopiers.

Gorbachev saw the books and balance sheets: the Soviet Union was running on 'empty'. He ordered the ministries to loosen their grip and allow limited local economic autonomy and small-scale enterprise. Calling for 'a second revolution of democratic progress', Gorbachev indicated to Estonia, Latvia and Lithuania that they should lead the way. They were in the vanguard because they ran their economies as well as was possible within an absurd system. The Balts had been sources of brain-power for the Russians for centuries. Although severely damaged by Soviet rule, they had not had the stuffing knocked completely out of them. They were better off than others in the Soviet net and retained a work ethic. If reform could not work in the Baltic lands, it could not work anywhere.

Taking Gorbachev at his word, the Balts saluted him as a reformer. 'Our angel', some called him. They were ready to run with the ball. But they quickly concluded that economic autonomy was impossible without a political equivalent. It was a burst of light. Tens of thousands of people pledged support for Baltic popular fronts founded to push for reform. They quickly became the dominant political influence, the focus of nationalist feeling. Many of their members and leaders were in the Communist Party. ('This is normal,' Peter said. 'They are not real communists.') Reformers in communist parties which had formerly been Moscow's rubber stamps told the Kremlin that times were changing. The old guard and the local KGB, brought up to jump on troublemakers, looked on in horror.

To much of the outside world the Baltic countries existed only in old stamp albums. Now the Soviet glacier was receding and the Balts were emerging and shouting 'Look! We did not die. We were here all the time.' Rallies filled the city squares. People sang patriotic songs as if believing that they could sing Moscow away in a Baltic version of Joshua's trumpets. There was a touching naïvety in the excitement, but the Balts had reached the heart of the matter. They showed Gorbachev that economic reform without a political dimension was impossible. The radicals saw with excitement and the hardliners with alarm that reform challenged ideology, that the Kremlin could not permit a more open society and simultaneously retain absolute authority and the canons of the faith. Power, privilege, legitimacy – everything was at stake.

Tall Hermann told the tale. On my next visit to Estonia Peter pointed to the flag flying from the flagstaff of the medieval tower standing sentry over the city of Tallinn. 'Look,' he said, 'we have our flag back and one day we'll get our country back. This is normal.' The people had hoisted the national tricolour and hauled down the hammer and sickle. They did not stamp on it or burn it. They solemnly folded it and presented it to the city museum, consigning it to history.

The Balts inquired into the forbidden past, prising out the truth about the secret clauses of the Hitler–Stalin pact, demolishing the Kremlin's lie that they had joined the Soviet Union voluntarily. They wanted their history restored to them, however grim, the blanks filled in. People had a hunger for history. A radio programme in which Estonian men and women reminisced was immensely popular. 'I was born in free Estonia,' said an elderly man, 'and I remember that we were craftsmen and worked hard. We were better off than the Finns across the water. There was plenty of food in the shops, wonderful cakes for sale.' Historians broke taboos and compiled recollections of the deportations in which the brightest and best, more than a half a million people, were rounded up and sent to exile and death. People remembered the trucks rumbling through the streets, carrying off teachers, farmers, businessmen and writers, anyone who could have provided leadership.

In a library in Tallinn I was shown some 'new' books on the shelves. They were old books: Stalin's secret police had swooped on the libraries, removing many of the books published in the years of independence, chopping them up with axes or burning them. Quick-witted librarians had hidden some in attics. Others, like the *Encyclopaedia Britannica* volumes dealing with Estonia and the Soviet Union, were officially committed to closed collections, stored away and marked with a green stamp. Half a century after their imprisonment I saw these books with their green tattoos, restored to the shelves.

The Kremlin, uneasy about the strengthening of the nationalist impulse, sent warnings and threats to the Balts. The Russian minorities in the Baltic countries grew anxious, too. Under Soviet Russification policies, large numbers of Russians were encouraged to settle in all the republics. They did not integrate, usually spoke only Russian and maintained an arrogant 'elder brother' attitude. During

Estonian independence the population was nine-tenths Estonian, but Russification has reduced the proportion to two-thirds of the 1.6 million people. In Latvia, Russians are more than a third of the 2.7 million people. Lithuania remains the most homogeneous, with four-fifths of its 3.7 million Lithuanian. 'No, we don't like Russians,' an Estonian writer said to me. 'They think themselves our masters and many of them are rough, uncouth and lazy. There are a few civilised ones; but overall we feel we are being swamped.' At Moscow's instigation Russians in the Baltic republics set up pro-Moscow movements to oppose local nationalism. The leader of the Russian group in Estonia said, 'There are millions of us. If they go on like this, the end will be bitter and three generations of Estonians will mourn.'

In August 1989, the fiftieth anniversary of the signing of the Hitler–Stalin pact, hundreds of thousands of people linked hands across the Baltic countries to form a 380-mile-long human chain. The authorities took no action. They had never been able to condemn the nationalists as young hotheads because the chief characteristic of the popular fronts was their maturity, a distinctly middle-aged appearance. 'As students in the 1960s, in the Khrushchev thaw, they had a taste of a freer atmosphere,' said Harry Tiido, an Estonian broadcaster. 'They feel they have a second chance that must not be wasted. They passionately want to achieve something for their country and don't want to spend their old age regretting that they did nothing.'

In Lithuania the commitment of the middle-aged has been exemplified by Vytautas Landsbergis, leader of Sajudis, Lithuania's Popular Front, who has found himself at history's cutting edge. A shy music professor, he seemed at first too mild a man to lead a nation, or to face Gorbachev and the Soviet might. He was the very picture of a prof, slightly stooped and bearded, blinking through wire-rimmed spectacles, laughing at his own jokes. He told me that the Lithuanian language was the core of his nationalism. He and his family had been involved in its development for more than a hundred years. His grandfather Gabrielus, a playwright exiled to Siberia for opposing Tsarist rule, had campaigned to make the language legal; and his other grandfather Jablonskis wrote the grammar that helped to establish it. His father fought for independence in 1918 and Landsbergis himself had made a particular study of the Lithuanian composer Miklayos Ciurlionis, whose music was banned by the KGB until 1987.

Landsbergis became leader because of his integrity and his unwavering view. 'If I had a short time to explain to Gorbachev how I feel about my country,' he said, 'I would say that Lithuania is beautiful but devastated and polluted; and all this has happened in my lifetime. Soviet socialism has damaged the Lithuanian spirit but not destroyed it. There are still people who know how to work and like to work. I am not afraid of what the Soviet Union may try to do to hurt us. I would be more terrified to learn that Lithuanians were ready to give up freedom.'

Gorbachev, pragmatic and apparently unperturbed, watched as Eastern Europe's communist regimes fell and the Berlin Wall came down. The Brezhnev doctrine of supporting communist governments had shrivelled. But at home Gorbachev defended as a central article of faith the Communist Party's pre-eminence. In the Congress of People's Deputies I watched him clash with Dr Andrei Sakharov on this issue. Sakharov had suffered for the ideal of a democratic Soviet Union and was a hero to the liberals. Gorbachev had freed him from exile. Frail and bent, his voice croaking, visibly reduced as a result of the suffering imposed by a spiteful state, Sakharov went to the podium to call for a multi-party system. Gorbachev, ringmaster in the congress he had invented as a democratic forum of sorts, replied testily and tried to shut him up. The following day Sakharov died. The democrats felt orphaned. Sakharov had borne the burden of being Russia's conscience as it groped its uncertain way out of the shadows. He had emerged from his brilliant scientific career to become the dissident of dissidents and an indefatigable foe of oppression. A quarter of a million people waited in bitter weather to pay tribute at his open coffin, to cast a flower on the bier, and their sense of loss was almost palpable. The official press which once reviled him praised his virtues.

Gorbachev went to Lithuania to warn its people not to rush towards independence. When a Lithuanian told him that after half a century of Soviet rule the shop shelves were empty, Gorbachev retorted: 'So shall we break up the union because of sausage?' He was surprised by the intensity of feeling for independence. From where I stood on a balcony in Vilnius stretched an historic tableau. In the background rose a tall Roman Catholic church, a focus of Lithuanian identity as well as of faith. In the middle ground stood a statue of Lenin, a crowd spilling through police lines and onto the statue's plinth to raise the Lithuanian tricolour. In the foreground, a trilby afloat in a sea of citizens, was the Soviet leader whose reforms had brought these people and himself to this crisis. He wagged his finger in his headmasterly manner. 'If you go for independence, you'll end up in the soup.'

That day, phlegmatic and orderly, the Lithuanians underlined their resolve with a huge rally calling on the Kremlin to return the country it took in 1940. The rally ended with fifteen minutes of silence. People thanked Gorbachev for having liberated words that were once imprisoned. They had cast off fear. I asked a woman in the crowd what she would do for independence. 'I'll go hungry and wear rags if necessary. We are tired of waiting.' Her daughter, aged eleven, was wide-eyed, filling the years of her growing-up with vivid and unforgettable events, more participant than spectator.

Within three months Lithuania declared independence and Landsbergis became president. The Kremlin responded by opening a war of nerves. Armoured columns rumbled through Vilnius and troops seized buildings. Gorbachev ordered a blockade to bring the republic to its knees. One sensed his anger in the words of the spokesman who referred contemptuously to Landsbergis as 'that music professor who calls himself president'.

Latvia was undeterred by the suffering of her neighbour. I went to Riga to see the parliament there declare independence. The following morning a group of us had a glimpse of how the other half lived. We breakfasted at an hotel in Riga which until recently had been the exclusive preserve of the Communist Party. It was utterly different from the run of Soviet hotels: no bullying doorman, no bored waitresses, no plates of cold peas and beetroot, no grime. Instead there were fresh, hot pastries, eggs and pancakes, proper coffee and smiling service.

Heading for Lithuania we bowled through a landscape of birch woods and meadows, brilliant with mustard, apple blossom and lilac, punctuated with windmills and dairy farms. Women worked in cottage gardens and men steered horse-drawn ploughs. We stopped to talk to a man and his wife waiting by the roadside. As soon as we mentioned independence, tears splashed down the woman's cheeks. 'I was like this last night,' she said. 'I was so happy I couldn't stop crying.' Her husband said, 'The Russians sent my relatives to Siberia. It makes me determined to get freedom. It's now or never.' Over the Lithuanian border a woman at a collective farm said, 'I'm glad the Latvians have joined us. You can break one branch over your knee but it is harder to break two.'

The blockade of Lithuania was having its effect. Petrol was scarce, but a man told me he had a steady source, a soldier in the Soviet army. In one of the hospitals Kes Vitkus, Lithuania's leading microsurgery specialist, said that the blocking of medical supplies had reduced his work to emergencies only. 'What Moscow is doing is not civilised,' he said, 'but it won't make any difference to our determination. I could not bear to live any longer under that terrible system. To hold back now would be a betrayal of my children. They can beat us and shoot us, but we will be free.' A café manager in the nearby town of Trakai said to me: 'For fifty years we have been ordered to do this, do that. As a boy I saw the mass deportations after the war. My father spent thirteen years in the gulag and when he returned he said not a word about it. He was afraid to speak. He has hidden it within himself. He is eighty-three and I want him to tell me, his own son, what happened. The communists closed our churches, uprooted our crosses. Many young people believe in nothing and expect the state to provide – this is the Soviet legacy. The blockade is a teacher. For the first time we have to take responsibility for ourselves, to face realities. It will help us rebuild our self-respect.'

In their hearts and minds these Baltic people had already left the Soviet Union.

★   ★   ★

At the Soviet Communist Party's 28th Congress most of the delegates were Russian and male. There were large squads of uniformed military men, the guardians of ideology. There were some Central Asians, the men with embroidered caps and the women in billowing iridescent dresses, reminding the Russians of the burden of empire. Most of the people were of like mind, party managers and local oligarchs, suspicious of reform, and the herd instinct seemed strong. When the clock struck 2 p.m. it was a mistake to be standing in the corridors, for that was when the Congress broke for lunch and delegates rushed for the eighty laden tables, one of the last of the great Soviet buffets.

Gorbachev rounded on the critics who accused him of giving in to the West and allowing communism to collapse in Europe. 'What do you want us to do – send the tanks? Teach them how to live?' On the subject of a possible coup he said that 'even if anyone is mad enough to consider it, nothing can be achieved by dictatorship.'

The hardliners in the party, the bureaucracy and the army brooded. The party had lost direction and people were leaving it in large numbers. The circulation of *Pravda* and all the official newspapers had slumped. The party was suffering death by a thousand cuts. The names of many towns and streets were being restored to their pre-communist versions. The country was breaking up and Gorbachev's decrees were ignored and could not be enforced. He bent with the wind to keep power, allied himself with the hardliners, and brought more anti-democrats into his government. Boris Yeltsin warned him of the perils of siding with the dinosaurs.

When the foreign minister Eduard Shevardnadze resigned, warning of an approaching dictatorship, the joy of the foes of reform was undisguised. Shevardnadze, who had been deeply troubled by the army massacre of civilians in Georgia, feared a military takeover. He had been under remorseless attack from those who hated his policy of rapprochement with the West. The hardliners believed that the tide was now turning their way. They yearned for the old order and ached to strike a blow.

Vilnius was sombre when I arrived on the overnight train that January morning. There was a sense of threat, as in the prelude to a thunderstorm. In the crooked streets and cobbled squares I did not turn a corner without seeing a Lithuanian flag.

I wondered how far Gorbachev would go to break the Baltic countries. The situation had all the makings of a showdown. People were convinced that the army planned bloodshed, and wanted to do in Vilnius what had been done in Tbilisi in 1989. They nevertheless rallied in Independence Square outside the parliament, singing patriotic songs and waving flags. The massive caramel cube of the parliament was the heart of things, the very symbol of independence. The people fortified it with barricades of vehicles, concrete blocks, wire and timber. Inside, hundreds of men in berets and baggy black overalls were ready, as one of them said, to defend the building with their fists. They tore out the metal rods that supported the balustrades to make clubs. Some carried old rifles and sporting guns. Others, in khaki uniforms that were replicas of those worn by the Lithuanian army before 1940, seemed to have dressed for an operetta. These unmilitary-looking warriors strode about trying to appear dashing. One of them, a playwright, told me his uniform had been made by a tailor in Vilnius. The presence of these men might have been comic, had not the circumstances been so desperate. 'For each man in this building there are ten outside ready to take his place,' I was told. I believed it.

Gorbachev sent an ultimatum: submit to Soviet law or face direct rule from Moscow. It was the toughest threat so far. Well, said the Lithuanian vice-president, the hour has come: we have to choose between independence and slavery.

Armoured vehicles moved around the city during the night. In the morning tanks arrived outside the press building where most of the republic's newspapers were produced. Troops smashed the doors and poured in. They wrecked the offices and kicked and bundled people out, dragging some by the hair. They opened fire and wounded two men. A crowd gathered around the tanks and demanded to know why the soldiers were attacking unarmed people. Women shook their fingers at the soldiers. 'Your mother in Russia would be ashamed of you,' they said.

A young man on a balcony directed water from a fire hose towards the soldiers below. An enraged officer grabbed a Kalashnikov rifle and we all shrank back as he raised the weapon, a few feet from us. His eyes were wild. He was out of control. He opened fire, aiming above our heads. Bullets struck the balcony sending chippings of concrete spattering down on us. People kept their nerve and stayed hunched together. 'Free Lithuania,' they shouted. The officer stalked off. The man on the balcony was brought down, a gaping bullet-hole in his face.

If the army expected to intimidate these people, they did not have their measure. Men and women, young and old, flocked to the press building to face the troops and sing songs. Several thousand had congregated when seventy soldiers charged, smashing rifle butts into faces and firing blanks into the thick of the crowd. The people could not know that they were not live rounds. Their dignity and bravery were impressive. The troops fell back.

That night thousands went to the parliament building to defend it with their bodies. Inside, men made Molotov cocktails and sandbagged the doors. Landsbergis called them together. 'We shall defend our freedom now or lose it again,' he said. The men raised their right hands and swore to fight for Lithuania. Outside the building people linked arms, swayed and sang. A crowd formed around a fiddler playing lively tunes. In the neighbouring square a pop concert began and people held hands and danced.

In the middle of the night we had word that tanks and troop carriers were heading for the television transmitter. It was not difficult to find somebody to drive a group of us correspondents: many Lithuanians wanted to play a part in getting the news to the world and would take no payment for running the risk of driving us around. When we arrived at the television tower the attack had started and tanks had rolled over cars, crushing them like cans. People had been killed and injured under the tracks. Hundreds of men and women joined arms in passive resistance, a human wall, singing songs. Soldiers fired at close range and bludgeoned people with rifles. There was wild shooting and heavy machine-gun fire. A battle tank fired a blank round into the crowd. Light tanks charged into the people, swerving to chase them as they ran.

I went to the hospitals. Fourteen people had been killed and 700 injured. I returned before dawn to the television station. Troops were sneering. Shrines were set up with candles, flowers and flags. Gorbachev dispatched one of his toughest generals to direct military operations in Lithuania, the man who had demanded Moscow rule and the overthrow of the Vilnius government. People feared the worst. Troops seized more buildings. As soldiers took over a radio relay station I asked an officer who had sent them. Jabbing his rifle into my stomach he said, 'Gorbachev'.

Earth-movers dug anti-tank moats around the parliament and cranes swung eight-ton concrete blocks to build walls. The defences looked medieval. People kept vigil, huddled around watchfires. The number of defenders in the parliament was reduced. The government believed the army would kill everyone inside, and that since Lithuanians had already proved they were willing to die for freedom there was nothing to be gained from an unnecessarily massive sacrifice. Everyone expected an attack and expected to be killed. I was moved by the quiet courage I found everywhere. In the nervous atmosphere in Vilnius word went around that the army would expel correspondents before attacking the parliament. A Lithuanian took a group of us into hiding in his home. It was a risk for him, but he wanted us to be witnesses. Perhaps international reaction persuaded Gorbachev and the hardliners to halt the killing. At his hospital the surgeon Kes Vitkus showed me the terrible effects of the blast when the tank fired its blank round into the crowd. As an expert in rebuilding shattered bodies, he had the closest possible knowledge of the price his countrymen had paid. Shortly after the attack on the television tower he and his wife Daisy, who had been married in a Soviet civil ceremony fifteen years earlier, married again in a Lithuanian church with their two children watching. It was a special kind of pledge to their country.

In Moscow a few days later I saw Gorbachev at a press conference. He was sweating. Anxiety haunted his face. People were saying openly that he was returning to hardline rule, redrawing the Iron Curtain. Gorbachev had called the conference in order to assert that he was in charge of the country and committed to reform. He blamed Baltic nationalists for the recent violence. He looked uneasy. Some of us later had dinner with Boris Pugo, the hardline Interior Minister who believed in putting down Baltic independence movements with force and who lied as naturally as he breathed. We ate meatballs, the finest I had tasted in Moscow, the meatballs of the privileged. Pugo gazed at us with his cold blue eyes and peddled the official version of what had happened in Vilnius, that those who died were victims of road accidents.

With hardliners in the ascendant, a chill beyond winter's cold fell over the country. Food shortages were severe and the government admitted to the worst economic figures since the war. High-value banknotes were suddenly abolished in a bizarre attempt to reduce inflation. Television reverted to the style of the Brezhnev era, presenting news fit for diehards. There was a battle for truth between the radical newspapers and the lying official press.

Army officers pressed for martial law in the Baltic lands. Hard-line mediocrities in the government, like the KGB chief Vladimir Kryuchkov and the prime minister Valentin Pavlov, revealed the desperation in the Kremlin as the crisis worsened by accusing foreigners of plots to undermine the country. There was a return to discredited ideology. The old guard rejected reform but offered nothing positive in its place. In an attempt to intimidate people the Kremlin ordered troops to join police on patrol in the city streets. Yeltsin, leader of the Russian republic, who had become a buffer between the hardliners and their ambition to wipe out the demo-crats, said that Gorbachev had 'lost his common sense'.

Gorbachev was isolated and deeply unpopular. All the reformers were elbowed out of the Kremlin and replaced by those who favoured the iron hand to bring the country to order: the military–industrial barons, farm bosses and local leaders who opposed reform and preferred the ramshackle but ideologically acceptable system they had been raised under. Tass wrote the epitaph of Gorbachev's reform programme, saying there had been a switch to a moderate–conservative approach.

The democrats battled on. Supporters of Yeltsin turned out by the thousands in Moscow to march for democracy and defy a Kremlin order banning the march. In an attempt to browbeat the people the Kremlin called out huge forces of troops and police and warned of the possibility of a bloodbath. But the people carried the day without any violence. The Kremlin bosses made themselves look foolish, clumsy, desperate and out of touch. Their bluff was called.

This same mediocrity, the second-rateness that characterised Soviet rule, was the distinguishing stripe of the grisly octet who sought to overthrow Gorbachev. In surrounding himself with such colleagues Gorbachev was like a man who fills a pool with crocodiles, jumps in, and wonders why he is bitten. The plotters were ready to countenance large-scale slaughter of innocent people, civil war and the ushering in of a new winter at home and abroad. Nothing was so revealing of the conspirators as their document of justification: hypocritical, incoherent, slobbering, without a single workable idea. It was a preposterous script. The attempted coup was evidence of the fragility of the Soviet Union.

The possibility of a hardliners' coup had often been talked of. Everything depended on the unity and sense of purpose of the plotters, the army, the party and the KGB. But unity was always in doubt and the conspirators did not know what to do. The army split across its political fault lines, between hardliners and reformers. The people took their destiny in their hands.

I believe there was a direct link between the January events in Vilnius and the drama in Moscow. In Vilnius, and in Riga, too, people had shown that they knew freedom lay in their own hands, had shown others how to defy and die. Many Russians were moved by such courage. Like the Lithuanians and Latvians they made their parliament their fortress and screwed their courage to the sticking place. Enough people broke from the ranks of the apathetic to make a fight of it. Enough soldiers threw in their lot with Yeltsin; and Yeltsin, springing onto a tank outside his stronghold, like Henry V on a wagon before Agincourt, seized history's moment in a physical as well as moral performance. People found in their hearts a noble indignation, the courage to say 'Enough!' to the empire of lies.

There was something of Rip van Winkle about Gorbachev when he returned. He was still prattling about the Communist Party being a vehicle for reform. He had not realised that the whole rotten structure, like a house eaten by death-watch beetle, had collapsed; that his policies were in ruins. It said much about the politician in this extraordinary man, and his sharp driving instinct for power, his compulsion to rule, that he dusted himself down, changed his coat, and sought a new role in the post-communist turmoil.

★   ★   ★

The next time I took the night train from Moscow to Vilnius it was a journey to a free country. Kes was beaming. He gave me a hug. 'It will be tough, but now we have a future and nothing can ever be as bad as it was.'

On the day of the August coup his hospital had prepared for the worst, for a massacre. 'We had seen the results of Soviet madness before, all the smashed bodies. We were right to be so fearful. After the coup collapsed a Soviet army officer told me that the soldiers would have wiped the Vilnius parliament from the face of the earth and killed and deported so many people that Lithuania would be silenced for a century. When the coup failed I was so full of emotion that I got my dog and we ran and ran and ran until we were exhausted.'

I went to the television tower. The Lithuanians who had taken over from the occupying Russians found the restaurant a stinking mess of chicken bones and bottles. Outside on the slope were wooden memorials to those killed in January, and on one a notice saying 'Father, don't forgive them, for they knew what they were doing.'

In a block of flats nearby I met Angeli Pladite, whose left leg was smashed when a tank rolled over her. She had already had six long operations in which surgeons grafted bone and tissue to rebuild the limb. She believed that she would walk within a year and she hoped that as she mended Lithuania would mend too – 'a whole country has to learn to walk.' She looked out from her balcony. 'I saw the tanks coming along that road,' she said. 'I joined a crowd of others running to defend the tower. The soldiers thought that shooting would frighten us but it had the opposite effect. We could all see in their faces that they had come to kill us. I do not feel bitter. It was my fate to be in that place at that time. I was born when Stalin's troops occupied our country and until two years ago I had no hope that freedom would come in my lifetime.'

I did not find a single Lithuanian who thought that independence would be easy. People had almost no idea of commerce, banking, modern agricultural and manufacturing methods and distribution. Economics professors had read the books but they did not know how a market economy worked. Economics aside, people had to make a huge psychological leap. They had to de-Sovietise their minds. They were like long-term prisoners thrown suddenly into the street, blinking in the light, nervous of the traffic, the world a strange and frightening place.

In the central park a demolition team was levelling the plinth on which the Lenin statue had stood, the statue at whose feet Gorbachev had laid flowers the year before. I was reminded of the felled statues I had seen in Moscow, of the horizontal Dzerzhinsky and Stalin's red marble body broken off from its boots, of Shelley's verse on the vanity of tyrants:

> . . . Two vast and trunkless legs of stone
> Stand in the desert. Near them on the sand
> Half sunk, a shattered visage lies, whose frown
> And wrinkled lip, and sneer of cold command,
> Tell that its sculptor well those passions read . . .
> And on the pedestal these words appear:
> 'My name is Ozymandias, king of kings:
> Look on my works, ye mighty, and despair!'

The jubilation that attended the chopping down of idols evaporated in the face of a future seemingly so full of shadows and ambush. The newly-free republics would have to find ways of living with the Russians; and Russia would have to make peace with itself. Its own nationalism was a resurgent and potent force. It was a tangle of contradictions, an expression of pride and disappointment, of a yearning for both rustic simplicity and greatness, of phobias and the politics of blame. It encompassed an incoherent muddle of democrats, anti-democrats, monarchists, mystics, religious groups, anti-Semitic ultra-nationalist blackshirts – and also communists and Stalinists, who scuttled off like cockroaches, hoping to survive, as cockroaches do.

History was on the boil. Russia had arrived at the end of the

twentieth century, a vast country of 147 million, spiritually de-
pleted, humiliatingly unable to feed itself. Its myths were deflated,
its legions stranded, and millions of Russian people confronted an
uncertain future as minorities in the old Soviet republics. In Moscow
men hoped to plant democracy in the old authoritarian soil. It was a
difficult and dangerous time. An unruly land entered a new age of
unruliness. To a greater or lesser extent we shall all have to share it
and endure it.

Index

Index